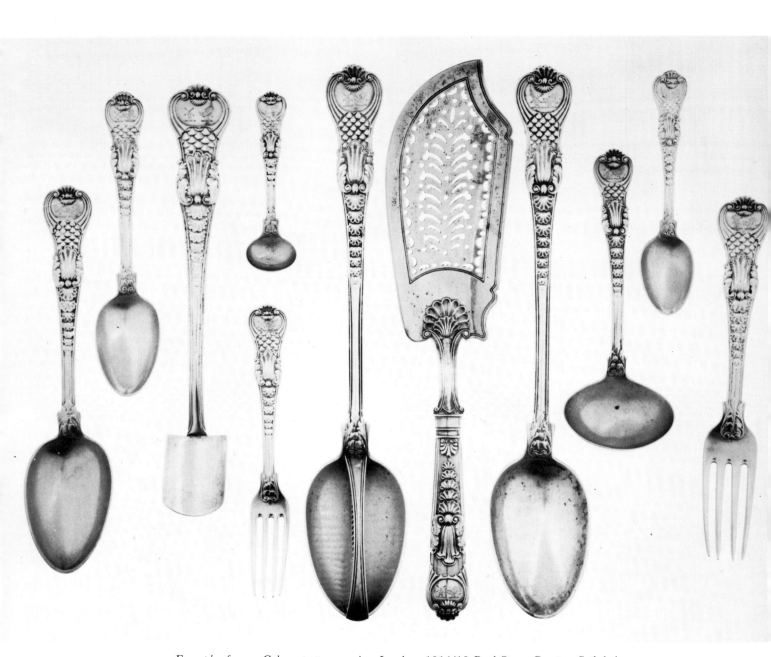

Examples from a Coburg pattern service, London, 1814/18 Paul Storr. Courtesy Sotheby's.

Silver Flatware

English, Irish and Scottish 1660-1980

Ian Pickford

Antique Collectors' Club

© 1983 Ian Pickford
World copyright reserved
First published 1983
Reprinted 1988, 1993, 1995

ISBN 0 907462 35 9

The right of Ian Pickford to be identified as author of this work has been
asserted by him in accordance with the Copyright, Designs and Patents Act 1988

British Library Cataloguing-in-Publication Data
A Catalogue record for this book is available from the British Library

Printed in England on Consort Royal Satin from Donside Mills, Aberdeen, by
the Antique Collectors' Club Ltd., 5 Church Street, Woodbridge, Suffolk IP12 1DS

The Antique Collectors' Club

The Antique Collectors' Club was formed in 1966 and quickly grew to a five figure membership spread throughout the world. It publishes the only independently run monthly antiques magazine, *Antique Collecting*, which caters for those collectors who are interested in widening their knowledge of antiques, both by greater awareness of quality and by discussion of the factors which influence the price that is likely to be asked. The Antique Collectors' Club pioneered the provision of information on prices for collectors and the magazine still leads in the provision of detailed articles on a variety of subjects.

It was in response to the enormous demand for information on 'what to pay' that the price guide series was introduced in 1968 with the first edition of *The Price Guide to Antique Furniture* (completely revised 1978 and 1989), a book which broke new ground by illustrating the more common types of antique furniture, the sort that collectors could buy in shops and at auctions rather than the rare museum pieces which had previously been used (and still to a large extent are used) to make up the limited amount of illustrations in books published by commercial publishers. Many other price guides have followed, all copiously illustrated, and greatly appreciated by collectors for the valuable information they contain, quite apart from prices. The Price Guide Series heralded the publication of many standard works of reference on art and antiques. *The Dictionary of British Art* (now in six volumes), *The Pictorial Dictionary of British 19th Century Furniture Design, Oak Furniture* and *Early English Clocks* were followed by many deeply researched reference works such as *The Directory of Gold and Silversmiths,* providing new information. Many of these books are now accepted as the standard work of reference on their subject.

The Antique Collectors' Club has widened its list to include books on gardens and architecture. All the Club's publications are available through bookshops world wide and a full catalogue of all these titles is available free of charge from the addresses below.

Club membership, open to all collectors, costs little. Members receive free of charge *Antique Collecting*, the Club's magazine (published ten times a year), which contains well-illustrated articles dealing with the practical aspects of collecting not normally dealt with by magazines. Prices, features of value, investment potential, fakes and forgeries are all given prominence in the magazine.

Among other facilities available to members are private buying and selling facilities, the longest list of 'For Sales' of any antiques magazine, an annual ceramics conference and the opportunity to meet other collectors at their local antique collectors' clubs. There are over eighty in Britain and more than a dozen overseas. Members may also buy the Club's publications at special pre-publication prices.

As its motto implies, the Club is an organisation designed to help collectors get the most out of their hobby: it is informal and friendly and gives enormous enjoyment to all concerned.

For Collectors — By Collectors — About Collecting

ANTIQUE COLLECTORS' CLUB
5 Church Street, Woodbridge, Suffolk IP12 1DS, UK
Tel: 01394 385501 Fax: 01394 384434
——————— or ———————
Market Street Industrial Park, Wappingers' Falls, NY 12590, USA
Tel: 914 297 0003 Fax: 914 297 0068

To Linda — my wife

Contents

Foreword

I am greatly indebted to Ian Pickford for so kindly asking me to write the foreword to this fascinating and erudite book on silver flatware.

In the years since the last war there has been an explosion of interest and learning in the arts. The world of antique silver is no exception and although several publications have appeared on the subject of spoons and forks there has, until now, been no comprehensive book on the subject.

In his preface the author rightly comments that *The Oxford English Dictionary* has no entry under 'flatware', indeed it is a word borrowed from our American cousins and until recently older dealers would refer to it as 'spoonware'.

The spoon has been from early times a precious possession in a family, recorded in inventories and wills, and it is from this single item that the whole range of patterns and different pieces as we know them today has originated.

The purchase of silver spoons and forks has always been fundamental in the creation of a 'good table', as evinced by the old bills illustrated, and even to this day it probably forms the most important purchase of silver in people's lives.

With the introduction of full length dies in the early nineteenth century there was a most dramatic increase in the variety of patterns made available to the public. It is interesting to note how many of these — 'King's, 'Queen's', 'Fiddle, Thread and Shell', etc. — are as popular today as when they were first introduced over 150 years ago.

As a small historical note, readers may be interested to know that when our family business came to take over the Francis Higgins dies at the beginning of the war my father was asked to advise which suites of dies or patterns should be kept and which should be sacrificed for steel for the war effort. This is the reason that it is no longer possible to manufacture some of the more obscure patterns previously in the Higgins range. It is also of interest to note that some thirty to forty spoonmakers were employed by Francis Higgins in the first quarter of the century, so one can imagine the enormous output.

A great virtue of this treatise is the excellent number of illustrations and I am sure it will be of great use to collectors and the general public at large to know what particular pattern or design they own or hope to purchase.

The concept of building up a 'mixed set' from individual items is still a possibility, rather like philately, but it is rather a dubious hobby, as a good straight set, be it second hand or antique, is a better buy in the long run. The demand for silver flatware remains strong and I only hope the price of the raw material will stabilise at a reasonable level after the fluctuations generated by the Bunker Hunt saga.

It is high time someone should have sought to produce a considered history of this intriguing subject. Ian Pickford must have been born, or blessed, with the proverbial 'silver spoon' and I commend his studies to all readers.

Richard Vander, London

Preface

Many writers have devoted a section in their books to the development of the spoon or have, on rare occasions, produced a complete work on the subject. With few exceptions such works have dealt almost exclusively with spoons up to the second half of the seventeenth century and have then dealt only cursorily with the development of flatware. Even *The Oxford English Dictionary* has not, as yet, included an entry for flatware.

It is the aim of this work to examine this hitherto rather neglected area and provide a reference to the many patterns that have been produced. To do this I have divided the book into two parts, the first examining the stylistic development, production and history of flatware and its makers; the second, a reference section, dealing with the patterns.

The first part will, I hope, be of use and interest both to the novice and also to those already well versed in silver, containing as it does much previously unpublished material and the answers to some long standing problems, such as the Coker-Cachart controversy. Some seven or eight years ago, when first working on the book, I had the idea of tracing master/apprentice pedigrees to see if such an approach would solve this particular problem. There can now be little doubt of Coker's importance as a spoon maker.

There have been other moments of great excitement, as, for example, when discovering a spoon maker's portrait or when a Darby's patent spoon was offered to me as an 'oddity' for a photograph just before completion of the manuscript. It was some fifteen years earlier that I had found Darby's specification for making spoons in the patent records and had given up hope of finding an example for the book.

The second part of the book, 'The Patterns', is basically a reference in which a large number of patterns and their variants are illustrated, many for the first time, while several 'lost' names, subsequently rediscovered, are also recorded.

Since most users of this section will be trying to find the pattern name for a particular example I have grouped the patterns under principal stylistic types. This I feel is more practical than an alphabetical order. (A full alphabetical listing of patterns and variants is given in the Indexes.)

The examples included in this section cover comprehensively the hand-forged flatware patterns from 1660 to the present day though, inevitably, some of the more obscure patterns and variants may be omitted.

I have shown only a selection of the machine-made twentieth century patterns to give an idea of the sort of designs that were, and in many cases still are, in production. The problem when dealing with these is the vast number of variations of the general type produced by different manufacturers, often using the same name on wildly differing patterns, or different names for the same pattern! The problem is made no easier by the number of 'exclusive' designs commissioned from manufacturers by retail outlets.

Serving pieces have been dealt with separately at the end of the section on patterns, as have more peripheral items such as caddy spoons, snuff spoons and picture back teaspoons. With these, since the pieces discussed do not form the main theme of the book, the object has been to give a broad outline of their development and to aid in recognition of types.

Flatware is for many people the most important purchase in silver that they will make. If the information and advice in this book helps them make a wiser and better choice its aim will have been accomplished.

Acknowledgements

First I must thank Mr. Richard Vander for kindly writing the Foreword to this work.

I am indebted to the Wardens of the Worshipful Company of Goldsmiths for their permission to quote from their records; also to Miss Susan Hare, Librarian of the Worshipful Company of Goldsmiths, and Mr. David Beasley, Assistant to the Librarian, for their help with the records. My thanks must also go to Mr. John Forbes, O.B.E., Deputy Warden of the Worshipful Company of Goldsmiths for his assistance with photographs of forgeries.

For her help in guiding me through the Wakelin Ledgers and for other invaluable advice I would like to thank Mrs. Elaine Barr, visiting scholar at the Victoria and Albert Museum.

For many thoughts and ideas exchanged over the years, and in particular for drawing my attention to the picture of John Lambe, I would like to thank Mr. Michael Snodin, formally of the Department of Metalwork, now of the Department of Prints and Drawings of the Victoria and Albert Museum.

The members of the Department of Metalwork of the Victoria and Albert Museum must also be thanked for their help, as must those of the Department of Prints and Drawings at the British Museum, the National Maritime Museum, and the Patent Office. I should also like to thank Molly Pearce, Keeper of Applied Arts, Weston Park Museum, Sheffield.

A special thanks must go to Cherry Lewis, my editor at the Antique Collectors' Club, whose help, patience and understanding have been greatly valued.

I would like to thank the members of various companies for their help and advice in assembling the patterns. In particular Mr. David Green of C.J. Vander Ltd., Mr. John Surtees and Mr. Putt both formerly of C.J. Vander Ltd., and Mr. Alan Kinsey of Bruford and Heming Ltd.

For their help in supplying objects for photography I would like to thank The Commercial Smelting Company, in particular Mr. S.A. Rote.

The following have generously helped with time, objects and photographs: Mr. John Bourdon Smith, Mr. James Charles, Mr. John Culme, Mr. Geoffrey Corbett, Mr. Stuart Devlin, Mr. Alastair Dickenson, Miss K. Hughes, Mr. Brand Inglis, Mr. Thomas Lumley, Mrs. M. McAleer, Mr. Michael McAleer, Mr. Lawrence Perovetz, Mr. Eric Smith, Mr. Peter Waldron, Mr. Henry Willis.

My thanks also go to the following companies for photographs and other assistance: Asprey & Company Ltd., Bruford and Heming Ltd., C.J. Vander Ltd.

I am greatly indebted to the following for the large number of photographs which they so generously supplied: Messrs. Christie, Manson & Woods Ltd., Messrs. Phillips, the International Fine Art Auctioneers and Messrs. Sotheby & Co.

I would also like to thank Sotheby's Belgravia for permission to reproduce their photographs.

For their time spent photographing the Hayter portrait, my thanks go to Mr. Tony Hunt and Mr. Robin Drake, both of B.B.C. Bristol.

I should also like to thank The Regency Press and Mr. A.C. Edwards for their help with the Mildmay Accounts.

The following individuals have all contributed valuable information and help in other ways: Mr. Jonathan Beagley, the descendants of William Chawner, Mr. and Mrs. A. Davey, Mr. B. Greenhill, Mr. David Hayter, the descendants of Thomas Hayter, Mr. Peter Maxwell Stuart, Mr. J. Parry-Wingfield, Mr. J.M. Perkin, Mr. Simon Spero, Dr. R.L. Tyson, Mrs. Fulford Williams.

I would also like to thank the photographer Mr. Peter Gates.

Finally I should like to thank the various members of the Antique Collectors' Club who over the years have written to me concerning flatware, as well as my university and I.L.E.A. students and the various members of the National Association of Decorative and Fine Arts Societies attending my lectures, all of whom have asked the pertinent and searching questions which have helped me write this book.

Part 1

Introduction

Services

The term flatware as applied today usually refers to services of silver spoons and forks. In its wider sense, though, it also includes such objects as plates and dishes, these being flat as opposed to hollow; hollow-ware is best illustrated by coffee pots, tankards and cups.

Flatware services are a comparatively recent introduction in the history of English silver, developing from the late seventeenth century as a result of the return of the court from exile, an event which had two major influences on the development of flatware. First, the introduction of the fork as a major eating implement. Although forks had been known and used much earlier, and were well in use on the Continent, it was not until this time that their use became more common in England and that they were made in sets with spoons.

Secondly, a change in etiquette took place, which required a table to be set with the necessary knives, forks and spoons, instead of each individual bringing his own knife and spoon.

The spoon had undergone important changes during the mid-seventeenth century, from the Early English form (Figure 1) through the Puritan (Figure 2) to the Trefid (Figure 3), and with the introduction of tea and coffee, desserts and condiments, the spoon began to be made in a much greater variety of sizes.

Fashion, of which all of these changes could be said to be a part, then demanded the destruction of the old and the obsolete and their replacement with the new, which included sets of spoons and forks of a unified design, from condiment to basting spoon, from spice to table fork. And so the first flatware services were produced.

What then constitutes a flatware service? For the purposes of this work the generally accepted trade definition will be used. On this basis a flatware service will consist of:

12 table spoons	12 table forks	12 tea/coffee spoons
12 dessert spoons	12 dessert forks	

Knives have been omitted from this list because they are normally considered separately from flatware itself; strictly speaking, knives are not flatware at all but cutlery. The principal reason, however, for their exclusion is that original knives are seldom found with any service made much before the end of the nineteenth century, and it is an accepted practice today to purchase modern knives to match an old service.

More about this and the problems of old knives will be found in the section on Knives (see below pp. 46-53).

The term 'table' when used with either spoons, forks or, for that matter, knives requires some explanation. In the case of forks and knives these are the large size used for main courses, which included fish. The table spoon was for soup. Today many

Figure 1. *Examples of Early English seal top spoons. Private collection.*

Figure 2. *Six superb Puritan spoons made by Stephen Venables in London between 1653 and 1671. Courtesy Sotheby's.*

Figure 3. *Six Trefid spoons, London 1682; maker's mark is crowned (attributed (Kent) to John Smith). Courtesy Sotheby's.*

people use table spoons as serving spoons although they were never originally intended to be used in this way.

Why table? The term has been used from at least the first half of the eighteenth century. Before this spoons and knives had been personal objects carried by an individual to any banquet, even with the King. For the first time now services were produced to be set on the table, hence they were referred to as table spoons, forks or knives.

The word 'dessert' in itself does not require any special explanation. As with table spoons and forks it has been applied from the earliest production of flatware. What is important is that during the eighteenth century dessert spoons, forks and knives were frequently produced in services which were separate from the principal table service.

Such dessert services were often of an individual design which did not match the contemporary flatware patterns. There were, therefore, fewer dessert size spoons and forks produced of any one pattern than the table size. It is for this reason that dessert spoons and forks can be such a problem when building a flatware service today.

The idea of separate dessert services was retained throughout the nineteenth century but finally lost its popularity at about the time of the First World War.

Tea, or coffee, spoons have been included in the basic service. As with the dessert size these were also produced in individual designs throughout the eighteenth and nineteenth centuries.

Figure 4. *Worcester printed blue and white coffee can, c.1765, 2¼ ins. high; Worcester painted blue and white teabowl and saucer, c.1755, saucer 4¾ ins. diameter. Courtesy Simon Spero.*

A point seldom realised is that teaspoons were smaller than coffee spoons during the eighteenth century and the explanation for this is easy to see. Tea was more expensive than coffee and was drunk from bowls which were about half the size of the coffee cans then in use (Figure 4).

Serving pieces are not included in the basic service. These are regarded as extra to any service and are examined under their respective headings (pp. 178-201). When determining the desirability and value of any service it is obviously necessary to take account of such serving pieces as may be present.

Fish eaters are a comparatively modern addition, and are generally found from the second half of the nineteenth century and onwards. They have, therefore, been omitted from the basic service and are regarded as extras (see Fish Eaters, pp. 205-6).

Egg spoons will be found with services but so infrequently that these, too, have been treated as extras (see Egg Spoons, pp. 204-5).

Having examined the reasons for the inclusion of the particular types of spoons and forks in a basic service, what of the numbers of each?

The convention today is to regard a service as being of twelve pieces of each type. There is of course nothing to stop anyone having either smaller or larger quantities than this.

With the smaller households of today services of six or eight are frequently found, while at the other end of the scale services which run into a thousand or more pieces have been made.

The norm, though, when talking about flatware, is to regard a service as being of twelve of each of the objects listed on p. 13. Should there be only six of each this would be referred to as a half service, twenty-four of each would be referred to as a double service, and so on.

Part Service

Another phrase may be encountered when examining services. This is a 'part service'. The expression refers to an incomplete or partial service as illustrated below:

Service	Part service
12 table spoons	11 table spoons
12 table forks	9 table forks
12 dessert spoons	10 dessert spoons
12 dessert forks	3 dessert forks
12 tea/coffee spoons	6 tea/coffee spoons

The value of a part service is going to be greatly affected by which particular parts are missing. The dessert size is the most important factor. As an example, take two part services of the same pattern, date and condition:

Part service A	Part service B
3 table spoons	12 table spoons
3 table forks	12 table forks
12 dessert spoons	3 dessert spoons
12 dessert forks	3 dessert forks
6 teaspoons	6 teaspoons
36 pieces	36 pieces

A and B both have the same total number of pieces, but part service B will be heavier than part service A and therefore will have the great bullion value. However, of the two, part service A, having a complete set of the dessert size, will be worth about half as much again as part service B.

Straight Service

A straight service is one in which all the pieces were made at the same time by the same person or manufacturer. Naturally the older the service, the less chance there is of it having survived intact. As a result, straight services command a premium.

There are two types of straight service: the straight original service and the straight assembled service.

The most sought after is the straight original service where all the pieces have always been together as one service and have probably been passed down through one family. Such a service will normally be engraved with family initials or crests.

The second category, the straight assembled service, has been matched by patient dealers or collectors over a period of time. Although all the pieces will be of the same date and maker they will only recently have been together as a service. A good many straight assembled services have been built from part services.

There are certain points to look for to determine whether a straight service is original or assembled.

First, is the service crested, initialled, etc. If it is, do all the pieces look as though they have been engraved by the same hand? If not, then the service will certainly be assembled. If they are all by the same hand, is it an old or modern engraving? (see Engraving p. 66). Are there signs of any previous crests or erasures under the existing crest? Remember here that some original services have changed families in the past and have had their crests or initials changed.

If the service lacks any crests or initials this generally indicates an assembled service. Look for signs of erasure (see p. 66). Few eighteenth or nineteenth century services have survived to the present day without being engraved with some form of identification. Bear in mind that families falling on hard times and having to sell their plate have frequently required their crests to be removed before such a sale.

Another point to look for is any abnormal variation in the condition of the pieces throughout the service.

Finally look at the journeyman's marks (see p. 44) which will be found on most flatware from the late eighteenth to the early twentieth centuries. With straight original services the same mark will appear on all the pieces. In some cases one journeyman's mark will be found on all the spoons and another's on all the forks. With assembled services quite a few different journeyman's marks will be found.

Mixed Service

A mixed service, as the name implies, is one in which all the pieces are of the same pattern but are of varying dates and makers. Its value will depend on the degree of variation.

A mixed service made by the same maker whose dates range over a period of, say, ten years is going to be almost as valuable as a straight service. At the other extreme, a service where practically every piece is of a different date and by different makers is going to be worth considerably less.

There are various ways in which mixed services have come about.

The first results from the unfortunate practice of splitting flatware services between the members of a family — a practice which should certainly be discouraged; it is far better to let one child have the complete flatware service and another the tea and coffee service than to spoil each by splitting them both. However, if the service has been split, then each child having a part of the service would order pieces to complete their own part. With the next generation the whole process is repeated, resulting in a service in which all the pieces have the same crest, but three or four dates and probably a similar number of makers.

Most mixed services today come either from a dealer specialising in flatware, who will build a service over a period of time, or a private individual doing the same thing over a generally longer period of time. The quality of both vary considerably.

Many dealers employ the unfortunate practice of automatically erasing and then polishing such services to a mirror finish. At best such dealers give them a 'butler' finish in an attempt to make them look old. Nothing, however, but time can replace patina.

It would surely be much better to leave such services with an honest mix and let the purchaser decide whether the pieces should be touched.

Part Straight Service

The expression part straight service, as distinct from part service, is sometimes used to describe a complete service of twelves in which a good number of the pieces are of the same date and maker.

Mixed Part Service

The term mixed part service is used to describe incomplete services of mixed dates and makers.

Stylistic Developments

Having examined what constitutes a service, and the particular descriptions which may be given to it as regards its composition, let us look at the principal stylistic developments and some of the possible reasons for these.

As we have seen above, flatware effectively came into being at the end of the seventeenth century. The Trefid (pp. 74-9), the pattern of this period, had come to us from France. As a result, the French manner of setting the pieces on the table was used. The spoons were placed open bowl down on the table and the forks were laid in a similar manner.

There were two important consequences of this. In the first place, crests and other means of identification were engraved on the backs of stems or handles, thus enabling them to be seen when the table was set. Secondly, the ends of the stem turned up — in other words towards the diner when viewed from the front. This allowed the piece to sit steadily on the table.

Both these features, engraved stem backs and turned up ends, are found throughout the first hundred years of flatware, i.e. c.1670-c.1770 and are found with the Trefid, Dog Nose and Hanoverian patterns (see pp. 74-94).

The forks throughout this period, with only rare exceptions, have three prongs or tines.

Important changes took place in the 1750s and 1760s. The ends of the handles of spoons were turned in the opposite direction, and crests, etc., were now engraved on the front of the stem and the spoons were placed on the table open bowl up.

Forks also changed at this time (c.1760), acquiring a fourth prong. In the majority of cases forks continued to turn up at the end as their three-pronged predecessors had done. The reason for this was a practical one — it is very uncomfortable to eat with a 'turned down' fork.

It would appear that forks continued to be placed on the table back uppermost since engraved crests and initials continued on the backs through to the mid-nineteenth century. From then on forks are found engraved on either the back or the front.

The next fundamental change — straight ends to stems — took place with the new flatware forms produced from about 1900 to the present day. With flatware produced after 1950 there has been a return to the use of three prongs for forks.

To summarise the basic developments discussed above:

Approximate datelines	Spoons Top of stem	Forks Top of stem	Forks Number of prongs
c.1670-1770	Turn up	Turn up	3
c.1760-c.1900	Turn down	Turn up	4
c.1900 and on	Straight	Straight	4
1950 to date	Straight	Straight	3

This is not, of course, to say that all examples will fit rigidly into this framework. All, and various combinations of, the above are being produced today. But the framework does help to place particular patterns in their periods.

Within this framework other important changes should be noted. We have already seen with turned-up end flatware that this encompasses the three principal early flatware patterns, i.e. Trefid, Dog Nose and Hanoverian.

The same applies to turned-down end flatware. In this group we have principally Old English and its variants or derivatives introduced in the second half of the eighteenth century, together with the Fiddle pattern and its derivatives which dominated the flatware of the nineteenth century (see table below).

Approximate datelines	Turned up	Turned down
c.1670-1700	Trefid	—
c.1700-10	Dog Nose	—
c.1710-70	Hanoverian	—
c.1755-1800 and to date	—	Old English and variants
c.1800-c.1910	—	Fiddle pattern
c.1805-to date	—	Fiddle based patterns

The vast majority of flatware patterns to be found today are based on either the Old English or Fiddle pattern.

Hand Made or Machine Made?

It is very important to be able to distinguish between hand-made and machine-made flatware.

Methods of speeding up the production of flatware were already being devised in the eighteenth century. In 1785 William Darby, a silversmith of Sheffield, patented a 'new method of manufacturing spoons and other articles'. His specification is shown below:

A.D. 1785 . . . . . . Nᵒ 1509.

Making Spoons.

DARBY'S SPECIFICATION.

TO ALL TO WHOM THESE PRESENTS SHALL COME, I, WILLIAM DARBY, of Sheffield, in the County of York, Silversmith, send greeting.

WHEREAS His most Excellent Majesty King George the Third did, by His Letters Patent under the Great Seal of Great Britain, bearing date the Tenth day of November, in the twenty-sixth year of His reign, give and grant unto me, the said William Darby, His especial licence that I, the said William Darby, during the term of years therein expressed, should and lawfull might use, exercise, and vend, within England, Wales, and the Town of Berwick-upon-Tweed, my Invention of "**A NEW METHOD OF MANUFACTURING OF SPOONS AND OTHER ARTICLES;**" in which said Letters Patent there is contained a proviso obliging me, the said William Darby, under my hand and seal, to cause a particular description of the nature of my said Invention, and how the same is to be performed, to be inrolled in His Majestie's High Court of Chancery within one calendar month after the date of the said recited Letters Patent, as in and by the same, relation being thereunto had, may more fully and at large appear.

NOW KNOW YE, that in compliance with the said proviso, I, the said William Darby, do hereby declare that my said Invention is described in manner following, that is to say:—

The silver plated or other metal being rolled through mills, as for other purposes, or hammered to the thickness of the thickest part of the spoon, sugar tongs, or spoon forks, it is cut with a bed and punch in the form of the article intended, and about a fourth part shorter than the dye in which it is to be stamped; it is then rolled at each end, but not at the middle, so as to bring it to the length of the dye by thinning each end as much as wanted, which must vary according to the weight upon the spoon or other article intended, which can only be ascertained by the judgment of the workman; they are then stamped with a hammer, stamp, screw press, or any engine of sufficient force, between two steel dyes, one or both of the dyes having the exact form of the spoon or other article intended. If they are large they are better struck hot of a dark red, if small they may be stamped cold. If the spoon or other article is stamped flat and raised afterwards, then the impression must be only on one dye, the other being quite flat; if stamped in the raised form, then the impression must be on both dyes, one forming the back, the other the front of the article. In stamping there will be superfluous metal squeese out between the two dyes, which is cut off by a bed and punch in the manner they are first cut out of the piece, but that the bed and punch must be the exact outline of the dye in which they are struck. If the spoons are stamped flat, the bowles must be raised by means of a convex punch the form of the bowl of the spoon forced in a piece of lead or pewter by a screw press or with a hammer, and after the pewter has received the form of the punch, the spoon is placed between the punch and pewter and receives its form by press or hammer. The same process serves for the sugar-tong ends for raising them as does for the bowls of the spoons. The spoon forks after being struck the first time, as described for the spoons, have the prongs pierced out with bed and punch, and then struck the second time; they then have the edges filed. The spoon and tongs when struck the second time just to put them in form, are filed on the edges of the bowl and handle, and the forks are done the same, after which they are burnished or polished as wanted. In the said articles made of plated metal, the edges must be turned over with a burnisher, or be tinned or have silver solder run on them to cover the bare edges of the metal.

The above description I conceive is sufficient for any person to make them by who are used to the working of stamps and cutting presses.

In witness whereof, I, the said William Darby, have hereunto set my hand and seal, this Sixth day of December, One thousand seven hundred and eight-five.

WILL<u>M</u> DARBY. (L.S.)

Signed and sealed by the said William Darby, being first duly stampt, the several inter-lineations between the 13th & 14th lines, the 14th & 15th lines, the 16th & 17th lines, the 17th & 18th lines, the 23d & 24th lines, the 24th & 25th lines, and the 26th & 27th lines, and the erazure in the 12th line, being first made, in the presence of us,

THO^S SHINBOURN.
GODF^Y FOX.

AND BE IT REMEMBERED, that on the Sixth day of December, in the year of our lord 1785, the aforesaid William Darby came before our said Lord the King in His Chancery, and acknowledged the Specification aforesaid, and all and every thing therein contained and specified, in form above written. And also the Specification aforesaid was stampt according to the tenor of the Statutes made for that purpose.

Inrolled the Ninth day of December, in the year of our Lord One thousand seven hundred and eighty-five.

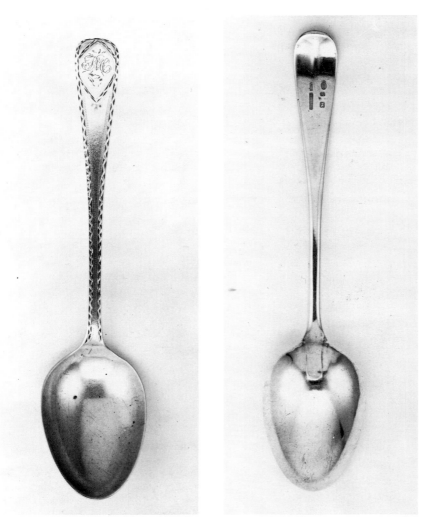

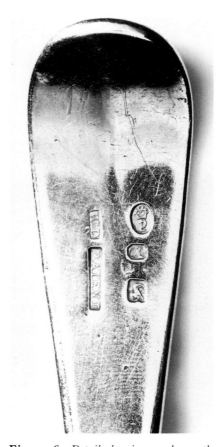

Figure 5. *The front and reverse of a bright-cut Old English pattern table spoon made by William Darby of Sheffield in 1785 using his patent method. Courtesy Henry Willis.*

Figure 6. *Detail showing marks on the spoon in Figure 5, 'PATENT' being stamped next to Darby's maker's mark. Courtesy Henry Willis.*

Darby's method differs little from modern machine production but, judging by the rarity of surviving examples, met with little success in the eighteenth century. An example of his work and his patent mark are shown in Figures 5 and 6.

It was not until the middle years of the nineteenth century that the Sheffield manufacturers started to mass-produce flatware on a large scale. Therefore any flatware prior to 1840 will almost certainly be hand made.

But what of flatware after 1840? Here we have a very useful and quick guide. The centre for machine-made flatware was Sheffield, for hand-made — London. Most provincial centres such as Exeter and Newcastle continued to produce hand-made flatware although little is found after 1850. A quick look at the assay mark will therefore give a pretty good idea as to whether it is likely to be hand made or not.

The place of assay and date of the flatware, although a useful guide, is not an absolute guarantee. How then can a positive distinction be made?

The test is a simple one. Take a piece such as a table spoon or fork and, holding it in the centre of the stem in two hands with thumbs pushing up, try to bend it. If it is hand made it will feel like a piece of sprung steel, if machine made it will readily start to bend. Once a piece has just started to yield it is unnecessary to take the test any further. Remember to restore the slight bend you have made — and to obtain the consent of the owner before you embark on this test.

Why is it so important to be able to distinguish hand from machine made? The answer is simple, to be able to judge quality and durability.

The method of making a spoon or fork by hand is a lengthy one. The whole piece, taking a spoon as our example, starts as just one bar of silver. One end is first flattened (ultimately to form the spoon bowl) by hammering the bar directly on to a steel stake (anvil). The stem is then hammered in similar fashion and gradually the spoon takes shape (Figures 7 and 8).

It is not possible to work continuously on the silver with a hammer since it becomes

Figure 7. *The principal stages of hand-forged flatware making, from a rod of silver to a finished spoon by Richard Cook of Stuart Devlin. Courtesy Stuart Devlin.*

Figure 8. *The principal stages of producing a decorated (King's pattern) spoon by hand. Note that the decoration is stamped in the die (see Figure 10) before the bowl is shaped. Notice also the thicker front edge on the final spoon, both here and in the previous illustration. Courtesy C.J. Vander.*

harder with each blow and eventually can no longer be worked. The process of annealing then has to be carried out. This involves heating the silver until it is red hot and then immersing it in water, thus softening the silver and allowing it to be worked once more.

With each successive annealing the silver does not become quite as soft as it was the time before, and by the time a spoon is completed the silver will be much tougher than it was at the start. Hence the fact that it will feel like sprung steel when an attempt is made to bend it.

Another very important feature of a hand-made spoon bowl is that the edges of the bowl, which require the greatest strength, are deliberately thickened during the forging process. The edges are thicker than the bottom and the front edge is the thickest of all (Figures 7 and 8).

When a spoon or fork is stamped on a machine there are no repeated hammerings and annealings to harden the metal. The bowls of spoons are of uniform thickness lacking the subtlety of the hand-made example (Figure 9).

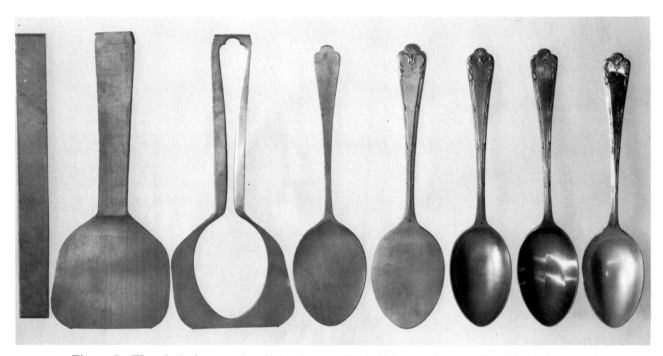

Figure 9. *The principal stages of producing flatware (Louis XVI pattern) by machine. Notice that the rod with which the operation starts is, unlike hand-made flatware, slightly longer than the finished spoon. The second stage shows the rod after cross rolling, the third the blank cut from the cross-rolled rod. Courtesy C.J. Vander.*

To sum up, the silver in a hand-made piece is much tougher than the machine-made example. Structurally the hand-made piece is also more durable, having greater thickness of metal where necessary.

It is for these above reasons that a two hundred year old hand-made service will often be found in better condition than one made fifty years ago by machine.

When purchasing absolutely modern flatware, a machine-made service will cost about two thirds of a hand-made example, but the hand-made will last for generations while the machine-made one will not. The extra expense of acquiring a hand-made service is always amply rewarded.

Die-stamping

Throughout the whole period of flatware production one of the principal methods of decorating pieces has been by die-stamping: lace back Trefids, picture backs, Old English Shell pattern, Fiddle Thread and Shell pattern and King's pattern are all examples of flatware where this technique has been used.

The decoration is first cut into a block of steel to produce the die itself (Figure 10), and to make any full service which requires die-stamping several such dies are required

Figure 10. *The two dies required to produce a double-struck (see p. 58) Rose pattern teaspoon, with the collar necessary to hold them in the correct position. Notice the slot in the collar through which the blank is inserted when the die is assembled. Courtesy C.J. Vander.*

to give a full range of size from salt to gravy spoon. Cutting the dies is a highly skilled operation and today very costly; dies are still being used which were first cut in the early nineteenth century.

Having prepared the die, the piece to be decorated is held firmly in it and hammered, forcing the silver into the decoration. Occasionally a double image may be seen, particularly with picture backs, where the piece has moved during the hammering process.

Today a screw press, or other mechanical means of applying pressure, is normally used rather than hand hammering.

Half dies are sometimes employed. With these separate dies are used for the top and bottom of the stem (Fiddle Husk pattern is still made using this method.) It is often the mixing of these that lead to some of the so called 'Bastard' patterns (see p. 72).

Flatware Makers

Spoon, and subsequently fork, making has always been a specialised branch of goldsmithing.

From the very start spoon makers were in trouble with the Goldsmiths' Company, as the following extract from the Company's records shows:.

Court of Assistants, 2nd July, 1663

At this Court complaint is made that the spoons which have of late years been made, and brought to the Hall to be assayed, have not been wrought for length and wideness of the boule as they ought to be, but much shorter in the handle, and lesser in the boule than heretofore; for remedy whereof it is thought fit, and ordered, that the form and pattern of a spoon shall be made and hung up in the Assay Office for the workmen to work thereby, and if any workman (after St. James's Tide next) shall bring, or cause to be brought, to the hall to be assayed any spoons of 2½ oz. or 3oz. weight otherwise made, the Deputy Assayer shall not receive the same, but shall return them to be new wrought again; which rule and order the Assayer is enjoined to observe and keep; and it is also ordered that a copy thereof be written, and set up in the Assay Office, to the end that workmen concerned may take notice thereof accordingly.

It is probable that the spoon makers were having problems with the stylistic changes taking place. In 1663 four important types of spoon were in production. Early English (particularly seal tops), slip tops, Puritans and Trefids, so it is no wonder that there were problems. What is most interesting is that a spoon should be made and hung in the Assay Office to act as a pattern for the makers. It is a fascinating example of the Goldsmiths' Company using their ancient rights to maintain high standards of craftsmanship in this country.

As regards the Goldsmiths' Company itself, spoon makers may be found amongst the lists of liverymen, members of court and wardens. It can, therefore, clearly be seen that to be a spoon maker was in no way to be considered a lesser member than, say, a large plate worker. Indeed the very highest position attainable in the Company, that of Prime Warden, has been held by such spoon makers as George Smith Hayter (1854 and 1863) and Henry John Lias (1861).

Both George Smith Hayter and his father Thomas Hayter are of particular interest, since they are amongst only a handful of spoon makers whose portraits are known (Figures 11 and 12). Thomas Hayter, who produced other plate as well, was apprenticed to, and subsequently partner of, George Smith II after whom he named his son.

Figure 11. *Thomas Hayter, citizen and goldsmith of London, partner of George Smith (1792), father of George Smith Hayter (see Figure 12) with whom he was in partnership from 1816; he died in 1840. Courtesy the Hayter family, Robin Drake and Tony Hunt.*

Figure 12. *George Smith Hayter at the age of 79 in 1872, son of Thomas Hayter (see Figure 11); this spoon maker was Prime Warden of the Goldsmiths' Company in both 1854 and 1863; he died in 1887. Courtesy the Hayter family.*

11

12

Figure 13. *'The Court of Equity or Convivial City Meeting' by Robert Dighton, 1779. Courtesy British Museum.*

Figure 14. *Detail of Figure 13 showing John Lambe the spoon maker. At this date he would have been in his late thirties.*

The earliest portrait known to survive of a spoon maker is that of John Lambe. He appears in a mezzotint dated 1779 entitled 'The Court of Equity or Convivial City Meeting' showing the interior of the Belle Sauvage tavern (Figures 13 and 14). At this date Lambe would have been in his late thirties and still working at 97 Fetter Lane, moving to number 29 the following year.

Up to the end of the eighteenth century the registers of makers' marks seldom refer to a goldsmith producing spoons as a spoon maker. When registering marks, most were entered as large plate workers and not, as might perhaps be expected, small plate workers. The names of most spoon makers have come to light by the simple evidence of their surviving spoons and forks.

Supporting evidence can sometimes be found. A good example is the record of the christening of Jane Sarah, daughter of Mr. Isaac Davenport in the registers of St. Vedast Foster dated 29th December, 1710, where Isaac Davenport is described as 'a spoonemaker in Gutter Lane'.

In 1773 a report was prepared for Parliament on hallmarking in England. An appendix to that report was published entitled: *An ACCOUNT of the Names and Places of Abode of all the Goldsmiths, Silversmiths and Plateworkers now living, that have entered their Marks in the Assay Office in Goldsmiths Hall, in the City of London,* London, March 8th, 1773.

What is not indicated by the above title, is that next to each workman's name is listed his trade (though in some cases trades are not specified). In this list may be found thirty-three individuals or partnerships designated as 'spoon maker' (see below):

Spoon Makers from 1773 Parliamentary report

Workman's name	Place of abode
Barrier, Abraham & Ducommon, Louis	Rathbone Place
Beaddle, Benjamin	Old Bailey
Bennet, Edward	Lombard Street
Bennet, Edward Junior	Corner of Tooley Street, Southwark
Chawner, Thomas	Pater Noster Row
Daintrey, Marmaduke	Hartley Row, Hants.
Devonshire, Israel	No. 125 Aldersgate Street
Devonshire, Thomas	Pater Noster Row
Dobson, Edward	Fleet Street
Evans, Thomas	Wood Street
Fearn, William	No. 75 Wood Street
Foster, William	Without Bishopsgate
Gosling, Richard & Joseph	Cornhill
Hearnden, Nicholas	Pick-ax Street
Jackson, John	Little Britain
Jarman, Samuel	Great Newport Street
Innocent, John	Little Newport Street, Soho
Irvine, John	No. 127 Minories
Lambe, John	Fetter Lane
Naylor, John	Charles Street, Bridgwater Square
Osborne, Jonas	No. 18 Little Britain
Penston, William	Noble Street
Roker, Matthew	Greenwich
Roker, Philip	Bishopsgate Street
Ross, Robert	Bell's Buildings, Salisbury Court
Salmon, Robert	Saint Martin's Church Yard
Simons, William	No. 6 Barbican

Smith, George	No. 110 Wood Street
Tant, William Junior	Haberdasher's Square, Grub Street
Tookey, Elizabeth	Silver Street, Wood Street
Tweedie, Walter	Hollywell Street, Strand
Weston, William	Silver Street, Wood Street
Wood, Christopher Fly & Filkin, Thomas	Battersea, Surrey

The above list, though useful, should not be taken as complete. James Jones, for example, is listed without trade but can be shown to be a spoon maker.

Spoon makers may also be found listed with other trade designations. There are, for example, two George Smiths entered in the list, one as a buckle maker, and the other as a spoon maker. Both in fact produced spoons, the George Smith listed as 'Buckle Maker — Hogan Lane' being the George Smith who was later in partnership with Thomas Hayter (although it should be said that this partnership produced a general range of silver, in which spoons were an important part).

Other spoon makers are to be found who were involved with buckle making. Perhaps the most interesting example is the important spoon maker William Eley, who took out a patent for buckles in 1784, examples of which can be found bearing the words 'Eleys Patent'.

As we have seen above spoon making was a highly specialised branch of goldsmithing. However, all trained goldsmiths should have been capable of producing a spoon or fork and many did. Examples can be found bearing the marks of some of the greatest goldsmiths such as Pierre Platel, Paul de Lamerie and Paul Storr.

In the second half of the eighteenth century an interesting group of flatware makers emerged. It would be a fair comment to say that the production of flatware at this time, and well into the nineteenth century, was dominated by members of the Chawner, Smith, Eley and Fearn families.

Not only were there many partnerships between the various members of each family, such as 'George Smith & William Fearn', 'William Eley & Willian Fearn', and, 'Williams Eley, Fearn & Chawner', they were also all connected in another fascinating way — that is through their apprenticeships (see table below).

A simplified table to illustrate the apprenticeship connections between the Eleys, Fearns, Chawners and Smiths

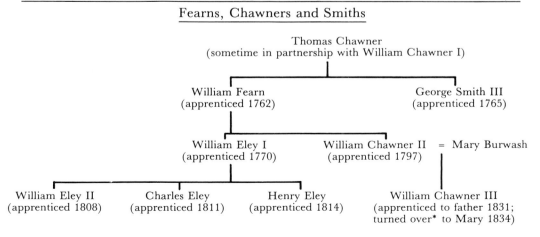

* Turned over is the term used when an apprentice is transferred from one master to another.

Spoon making as we have already seen is a highly specialised business; therefore, to become a spoon maker, it would be most logical to become apprenticed to a spoon maker. When George Smith was apprenticed to Thomas Chawner in 1765 it was to 'learn the art of a spoon maker'. Apprenticeships can, therefore, provide very useful evidence as to whom the spoon makers really were. By tracing the apprenticeship of known spoon makers back, finding the master of each and in turn his master, some fascinating pedigrees emerge. In most cases it is found that spoon makers follow generation after generation through these apprenticeships.

Coker or Cachart?

An examination of apprenticeships casts new light on the Coker-Cachart controversy. Both Ebenezer Coker and Elias Cachart worked in the middle years of the eighteenth century and registered similar marks at Goldsmiths' Hall as large plate workers (Figure 15). The most distinct variation between the two marks is that the top loops of the E and the C in Cachart's mark curl back through the letters whereas with Coker they stop short.

Figure 15. *Marks of Cachart and Coker.*   *Elias Cachart*   *Ebenezer Coker*

When a cursive EC mark of this period is found on a candlestick or salver it is generally said to be by Coker and when on a spoon or fork by Cachart.

There is no doubt that Ebenezer Coker produced both candlesticks and salvers; documentary evidence survives (the Wakelin Ledgers) to prove this beyond any question of doubt. However, to dismiss Coker as a spoon maker simply because the surviving ledgers do not show him supplying flatware to Wakelin is quite an assumption and, I would suggest, quite wrong.

If the apprenticeships of Ebenezer Coker are examined a fascinating picture emerges, as the following table illustrates.

Apprenticeships connected with Ebenezer Coker

A simplified table omitting apprentices whose subsequent freedom, marks or work have not been traced

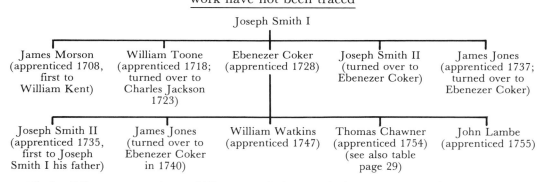

Joseph Smith I

James Morson (apprenticed 1708, first to William Kent)	William Toone (apprenticed 1718; turned over to Charles Jackson 1723)	Ebenezer Coker (apprenticed 1728)	Joseph Smith II (turned over to Ebenezer Coker)	James Jones (apprenticed 1737; turned over to Ebenezer Coker)
Joseph Smith II (apprenticed 1735, first to Joseph Smith I his father)	James Jones (turned over to Ebenezer Coker in 1740)	William Watkins (apprenticed 1747)	Thomas Chawner (apprenticed 1754) (see also table page 29)	John Lambe (apprenticed 1755)

All the fellow apprentices of Ebenezer Coker to their master Joseph Smith can be shown to have been spoon makers, as indeed can the apprentices of Ebenezer Coker. One of his apprentices, Thomas Chawner, became one of the most important flatware makers of the eighteenth century and, as can be seen from the table on p. 29, the whole Eley, Fearn and Chawner group evolves through him. Coker's apprentice, John Lambe (Figure 14) similarly ranks as one of the eighteenth century's most important flatware makers and came from a family of spoon makers. Why should the son of a spoon maker who subsequently became a spoon maker be apprenticed to a man, who according to some, never made a spoon in his life?

The above evidence helps in the identification of the master of Joseph Smith I. It is much more probable that he was the Joseph Smith apprenticed to Richard Overing in 1696 and who was turned over to the important spoon maker Benjamin Watts in 1700, than the Joseph Smith apprenticed to Richard Gutter in 1699.

On the basis of apprenticeships the most surprising fact is that Ebenezer Coker produced anything other than flatware. Salver making is, however, far closer in silversmithing technique than, say, coffee pot making. Candlesticks by Coker are cast — casting would be a necessary skill for a spoon maker.

An examination of the EC marks on spoons and forks reveals that these are indeed the work of Ebenezer Coker rather than Elias Cachart. Coker therefore and not Cachart must be regarded as one of the principal flatware makers of the mid-eighteenth century.

Chawner & Co.

Apprenticeship pedigrees solve many of the problems, others can be answered through family pedigrees (see table below). The Chawners are an interesting and, since they dominated the production of flatware in the middle years of the nineteenth century, an important family.

William Chawner (William Chawner II in the apprenticeship table on p. 29) the son of Jonathan Chawner a tanner of Horncastle, Lincolnshire, was apprenticed in 1797 to William Fearn. Some four years after completing his apprenticeship and receiving his freedom, in 1804, William Chawner entered into partnership with his former master, William Fearn, and his (Chawner's) fellow apprentice (although senior in apprenticeship by some twenty-seven years) William Eley I who had enjoyed a successful spoon and buckle making business for some time.

This partnership lasted until October 1814, Eley and Fearn then continuing on their own and Chawner registering his first mark in February 1815.

Chawner Family

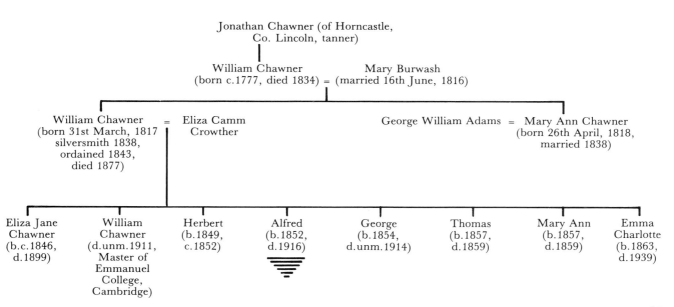

Jonathan Chawner (of Horncastle, Co. Lincoln, tanner)

William Chawner (born c.1777, died 1834) = Mary Burwash (married 16th June, 1816)

William Chawner (born 31st March, 1817 silversmith 1838, ordained 1843, died 1877) = Eliza Camm Crowther

George William Adams = Mary Ann Chawner (born 26th April, 1818, married 1838)

Eliza Jane Chawner (b.c.1846, d.1899)

William Chawner (d.unm.1911, Master of Emmanuel College, Cambridge)

Herbert (b.1849, c.1852)

Alfred (b.1852, d.1916)

George (b.1854, d.unm.1914)

Thomas (b.1857, d.1859)

Mary Ann (b.1857, d.1859)

Emma Charlotte (b.1863, d.1939)

It was in June of the following year, 1816, that William married Mary Burwash. Family tradition has it that the reason he married her was that she was a better spoon maker than he!

Their son William, born in 1817 and apprenticed to his father in 1831, would have been considered the natural successor to the firm. His training for this continued following his father's death in 1834 when he was 'turned over' (the term applied to the transfer of an apprentice from one master to another) to his mother. The widow, Mary Chawner, in turn registered marks in her own name and took over the running of the firm.

The young William Chawner completed his apprenticeship and received his freedom in 1838. All was then set for him to take over the running of the firm. William, however, had other ideas and entered the church, receiving his ordination in 1843 and becoming Vicar of Crich in Derbyshire, 1855-75 (Figure 16). The now Reverend William Chawner's younger sister Mary Ann had, in 1838, married George William Adams and it was he who then succeeded as the head of the firm, registering his first mark on 23rd November, 1840.

Figure 16. *The Rev. William Chawner, Vicar of Crich in Derbyshire (1855-75). Before being ordained in 1843 he had been apprenticed, first to his father William Chawner, and then to his mother Mary. He received his freedom of the Goldsmiths' Company in 1838. Courtesy the descendants of William Chawner.*

From this period on the mark of the company is that of George Adams, the company name being Chawner & Company.

Two fascinating discoveries have been made concerning the Chawners. The first is William Chawner's own flatware service (Figure 17) which is of the Fiddle pattern. It dates from about the time of his marriage to Mary Burwash in 1816. A precise date is not possible, since the pieces were never hallmarked but were struck with William Chawner's maker's mark only, once on each piece. William was taking advantage of the provisions in the Hallmarking Acts which allow pieces made for a goldsmith's own use and not for public sale to be exempt from assay. They were still required to be of the correct standard and to be struck with the maker's mark.

The other interesting discovery has been one of the Company's pattern books. It contains fifty illustrations (five to a page) representing some forty-seven patterns or their variants (see Appendix), and has proved invaluable in identifying some of the more obscure mid-nineteenth century patterns. It has also raised one or two questions over the correct nomenclature of some well-known patterns (see Albert pattern p. 140).

No date is given, but the pattern book must date from *after* 1862 since Napier is illustrated, the design of which was registered in that year, and before the 1880s when the company ceased trading.

Later Makers

Most of the important nineteenth century spoon makers such as Francis Higgins and George Adams were connected by apprenticeship or partnership with the Eley, Fearn and Chawner group.

After the middle years of the nineteenth century hand-forged flatware met with a serious rival, machine-made pieces. The machine-made product although quite inferior, as we have seen (p. 24), was markedly cheaper. Since 1850 the number of true spoon makers has steadily declined to the point where, in the 1960s, they could be more or less counted on the fingers of one hand.

The 1970s have seen an improvement in the numbers of master spoon makers,

Figure 17. *The Chawner family's personal flatware service. Made by William Chawner, possibly in 1816 at the time of his marriage to Mary Burwash. Notice that it has only a maker's mark, being made by a goldsmith for his personal use and not for public sale. Courtesy the descendants of William Chawner.*

largely due to the growing awareness of the importance of craftsmanship. One of the most outstanding of modern spoon makers is Richard Cook, a master craftsman working for Stuart Devlin (for his work see Figures 270-281). Having illustrated the portraits of earlier spoon makers it seems only fitting to end this section with a photograph of this great modern spoon maker (Figure 18).

Figure 18. *Richard Cook, a master spoon maker born at Bromley in Kent in 1942. Since 1968 he has been responsible for the making of all the flatware for Stuart Devlin. Courtesy Stuart Devlin.*

Women Spoon Makers

A good many of the known women silversmiths were spoon makers. The majority, such as Jane Lambe, were the widows of spoon makers simply running their deceased husbands' businesses.

Spoons were the finest products of (the today famous) Hester Bateman. The mark which she registered at Goldsmiths' Hall in June 1774 was as a spoon maker, and most of the earliest surviving pieces bearing her mark are spoons.

Goldsmiths' Bills

Surviving eighteenth century bills show very clearly how flatware was priced as well as the hard use to which it was put.

The account of Benjamin Mildmay, Earl Fitzwalter with Paul de Lamerie is fascinating in this respect. It runs from at least 1726 ('May 2nd, 1726, To Mr. Lamerie, silversmith, in farther part of his bill for plate. £100/0/0') up to the time of Paul de Lamerie's death in 1751 ('April 10th, 1752, Paid the executors of Mr. Paul de Lamerie, silversmith, in full of all accounts due to the deceased £40/15s/3d'). Below are extracts concerning flatware from the second of Paul de Lamerie's surviving bills with Earl Fitzwalter which is dated 1736.

Flatware extracts from a bill from Paul de Lamerie dated 1736

	£	s.	d.
To 12 knives, 12 spoons, 12 forks 47oz. 3dwt., 6s. 2d. per oz.	14	10	8
Fashion of the knives, 6s. per piece	3	12	0
Fashion of the spoons and forks 2s. 6d. per piece	3	0	0
Blades	1	0	0
Engraving		18	0
Case for them all	1	10	0

	£	s.	d.
To 2 spoons 4oz. 19dwt. at 6s. 2d. per oz.	1	10	7
Fashion 2s. 6d. per piece		5	0
Engraving		3	0
To a soup ladle, 8oz. 2dwt. at 6s. 2d.	2	19	11
Fashion 2s. per oz.		16	0
Engraving		1	6
To 8 skewers, 6oz. 10dwt. at 6s. per oz.	1	19	0
Fashion 3s. per piece	1	14	0
To mending a spoon		1	0

1731 July 12th

To mending a spoon		1	0

1733 May 22nd

To a large kitchen spoon, 3oz. 10dwt. at 6s. per oz.	1	1	0
Fashion		7	6
Engraving the crest and coronet		1	6

1734 July 19th

To mending 2 forks, adding 6 new prongs to them; they belonging to a travelling case		4	0

Oct 25th

To mending a spoon		1	0

1736 April 8th

To engraving a ladle		2	0
To mending a dessert spoon		1	0

In the contra account dated March 13th 1730/31
Received . . . . . & an old spoon 1oz. 12dwt. at 5s. 3d.

We do, fortunately, have another bill from Paul de Lamerie for another of his important clients, the Honourable George Treby, the flatware extracts from which are given below. It is quite interesting to compare the costs of Lamerie's two cased sets of dessert knives, forks and spoons (only the Treby account refers to them specifically as for dessert but, as will be seen, the weights, etc., are almost identical).

Flatware extracts from bills from Paul de Lamerie to the Honourable George Treby covering the period 1721 to 1725

	£	s.	d.
12 knifs, 12 spoons, 12 forks for desert, weighing 47oz. 12dwt.	15	1	5
Fashion of ye knifs, att 5s. each	3	0	0
Fashion of ye spoons and forks, att 3s. each	3	12	0
Engraving of all	1	10	0
Gilding of them all	6	6	0
Blades	1	4	0
Case for them	1	10	0
4 ladles or ragoos spoons, weigh 27oz. 10dwt.	8	14	0
Fashion 2s. per oz.	2	14	0
Engraving		6	0

Delivred 6 forks, at 13 shilling a piece	3	18	0
Engraving 9d. each		4	0
Case for them all	1	1	0

The above accounts illustrate quite clearly and independently that, in the 1720s, dessert services were being supplied separately from main table services.

The regular entries in Earl Fitzwalter's account 'To mending a spoon' indicate how casually such flatware was treated and explain a good many of the old repairs to be found on eighteenth century pieces. The most interesting entry, as regards repairs, in this account, is the adding of six new prongs to two forks. Three prong forks are amongst the most faked of all objects in English silver (see Pitfalls, p. 69). Finding such a fork today, with solder joins at the base of the prongs, one would dismiss it as a fake, probably as a conversion from a spoon, and yet here we have Paul de Lamerie 'adding six new prongs'.

The pattern is not mentioned in any of the entries. This is not at all surprising since effectively only the early Hanoverian pattern, with rat tail, was in production at this time.

Other early invoices and accounts are similarly vague as to pattern, using such phrases as 'newest fashion'. An account of Alexander Forbes of Edinburgh for the period 1700-5 includes the following entry for flatware made in 1702.

Extract from Alexander Forbes (Edinburgh) account
re flatware made in 1702

	£	s.	d.
Item for 18 newest ffashion silver hafts for knifes weighting 22oz. 9dwt. at £3. 4s. the ounce silver & £1. 16s. piece making	104	12	00
Item for 12 newest ffashion silver spoons weighting 30oz. 2dwt. at £3. 4s. ounce silver and £2. 8s. the piece making	125	04	00
Item for 6 newest ffashion forks 10oz. 8dwt. at £3. 4s. the ounce silver and £2. 8s. the piece making	048	00	00
Item for engraving your Lordships Crest on 36 pieces	018	00	00
Received 13 old hafts 18 ounces at £3. 4s. the ounce is	57	12	
Item ii Spoons & six forks all weighting 34 ounces 12dwt. is . . .	111	04	

The figures given are in Scottish £ s. d. of the period (in 1700 twelve Scottish pennies were the equivalent of one English penny).

The pattern of the 'newest ffashion' spoons (one of which survives) in the above account was the Dog Nose. One interesting comparison that can be made between Paul de Lamerie's charges and those of Alexander Forbes is that, whilst both charged for fashioning, Forbes bought and sold the actual silver at the same price whereas Lamerie was making approximately 1s. (5p) an ounce on the difference between his buying and selling price.

With the increase in variety of flatware during the second half of the eighteenth century bills and accounts start to mention specific features or patterns.

An invoice from Clarke & Green, which would appear to be a retailing firm, dated 27th July, 1787, is interesting both in this respect and in the composition of the service.

Extract from Clarke & Green's bill, 27th July, 1787

	£	s.	d.
Bo.ᵗ of Clarke & Green			
3 Double O'G inlaid Mahogany Knife Cases with threaded Silver Escutcheons & ect	5	11	—
3 Setts London fluted white Ivory table Knives with 3 Grain forks and silver ferrells	9	9	—
18 Pair D° Desert D°	3	18	9
2 Pair of D° Carvers D°	1	—	—
24 double threaded polished Silver table spoons double threaded each side . . . . .57..—	29	9	6
18 D° Desserts D°. . . . . .23..—	11	14	6
2 D° Gravy D° . . . . .6..14	2	17	10
18 D° Teaspoons. . . . . .12.. 3	6	—	10
6 fashionable threaded tureen Salts gilt inside & finished neatest manner . . . . .25..13	15	9	1
6 D° Ladles . . . . .3..—	1	14	6
1 D° Marrow Spoon . . . . .1..17		16	8

The first column of figures in the above extract indicates the weight of the item

There is an entry later in the bill for 'Duty' on 227oz. 2dwt. of silver at 6d., and another for 'Engraving 83 Crests on sundry &c. at 4d — £1 7s. 8d.'.

The flatware, part of which still survives, is Old English Thread. Notice that no silver forks were made for this service, all were ivory with silver ferrules. The word 'grain' ('3 Grain forks') could refer to the ivory being stained (usually green); however the entry above for the knives refers to them as 'white Ivory' and it would be odd to mix the two, but perhaps this is the case.

The composition of a service made by the early nineteenth century is well illustrated in the extract given below of a bill from Thomas & John Ollivant of Manchester dated 1836.

Manchester

Bought of Thomas & John Ollivant Silversmiths Jewellers & Watch Makers

					£	s.	d.
Decem 7	18	Husk pattern	Silver	Table Forks	26	4	—
	18	ditto	ditto	Dessert Forks	16	9	6
	18	ditto	ditto	Table Spoons	26	3	6
	18	ditto	ditto	Dessert Spoons	16	8	6
	18	ditto	ditto	Tea Spoons	9	12	6
	2	ditto	ditto	Gravy Spoons	5	12	6
	a	ditto	ditto	Soup Ladle	4	6	6
	4	ditto	ditto	Sauce do.	5	9	—
	6	ditto	ditto	Salt do.	2	12	6
	a	ditto	ditto	Fishknife	4	1	—
	a	ditto	ditto	Butterknife	1	8	—
	a pr.	ditto	ditto	Sugar Tongs	1	7	—
	a	ditto	ditto	ditto Ladle		17	—
	a	ditto	ditto	Caddy do.		11	6

It will be noticed that no mention is made in the Ollivant bill of fashioning charges. By the nineteenth century Ollivant was largely a retailer and flatware such as that mentioned in the bill would have been supplied by one of the large London companies. From the evidence of surviving flatware supplied in the nineteenth century by Ollivant (subsequently Ollivant & Botsfords) it is clear that George W. Adams of Chawner & Co. must have been their major supplier.

It will also be noticed that no knives are given with the flatware in the Ollivant bill. Later in the same bill is the following entry:

			£	s.	d.
3 dozen	Best Ivory Balance Table Knives at 32s.		4	14	6
1 "	.................ditto.................Forks				
	21s., 2 dozen do. Dessert Knives at 26s. 6d = 53s.		3	14	—
1 "	dessert Forks 15s. 6d. 1 pr. ditto Guard Carvers ea				
	10s. & 11s.		1	16	6
2 pair	ditto Game Carvers 9s. = 18s. Engraving crest on the				
	Silver 66s.		4	4	—

It is clear, therefore, that ivory-handled knives were to be used with this silver Husk pattern service. This provides us with another answer as to why original silver handled knives of matching pattern are so seldom found with services.

Hallmarks

It is not the intention of this work to give a detailed history of the hallmarking system of this country.

What is important is to see how, at various periods, marks were struck in different ways on flatware, and why these changes occurred, as well as to look at the overall pattern.

To examine this properly it is necessary to start in the first half of the seventeenth century. Fully marked London spoons will be taken as our examples throughout (for partial marking see p. 42).

Position of Marks

The changes in the positions of marks c.1650-1850 are shown in Figure 19.

The Early English form of spoon (Figure 1) was marked with the leopard's head in the bowl of the spoon and the remaining three marks (maker, lion passant, and date letter) struck together at the base of the back of the stem (Figure 20).

When slip top spoons (Figure 21) were produced a special form of marking was used. The difference to the conventional marking of a knopped spoon was that the date letter was struck near the top of the stem, quite separately from the maker's mark and lion passant. The reason for this was quite simple. If a slip top was marked in the conventional manner it would be very easy for an unscrupulous workman to add a finial, and thus unassayed silver, to the stem. By marking in this special way it indicated to the officials of the Goldsmiths' Company that the spoon was assayed without a finial.

Stump tops, Puritans (Figure 2) and notched end Puritans were all marked in this special way during the middle years of the seventeenth century. It was therefore quite logical in the 1660s to mark the newly introduced Trefid spoons in this way since they, too, had no added finial.

With the Trefid came a marking problem. The problem resulted from the rat tail which now appeared on the back of the bowl, making it no longer possible to strike the leopard's head in the bowl. The solution was a simple one, the leopard's head was moved to join the maker's mark and lion passant at the base of the stem.

Having established how the marks came to be positioned in this rather odd way on the earliest true flatware (three at the bottom and one at the top of the stem), the reason for the changes in the positioning of the marks during the last quarter of the seventeenth century are easier to understand.

With the establishment of the Trefid as the principal pattern of the late seventeenth century few knopped spoons were produced. The fact that the Trefid had a distinctive shape at the top of its stem made it most unlikely that anyone would add a finial. The necessity for the special, slip-top type of marking therefore ceased.

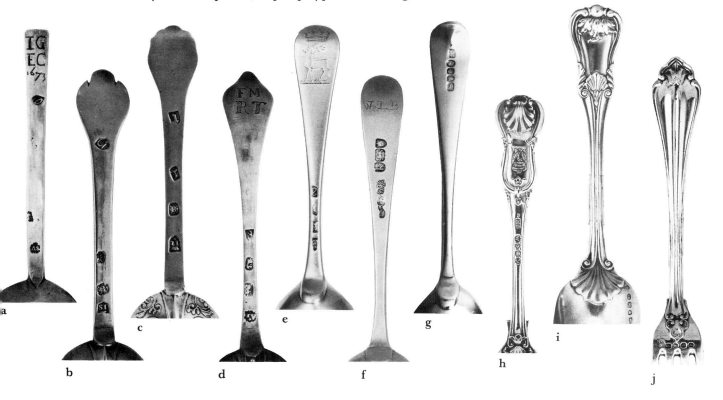

Figure 19. *Changes in the positions of marks c.1650-1850. All London. Left to right:*
a. *1655. Slip top and Puritan marking, maker's mark and lion passant bottom of the stem, date letter at top (leopard's head passant in bowl). Courtesy Sotheby's.*
b. *1671. Early Trefid marking, maker's mark, lion passant and leopard's head bottom of stem, date letter at the top. Courtesy Phillips.*
c. *1686. Middle period Trefid marking, marks spread evenly along stem. Courtesy Sotheby's.*
d. *1704. Late Trefid and Dog Nose marking, marks grouped at bottom of stem. Courtesy Phillips.*
e. *1736. Bottom marking. Courtesy Phillips.*
f. *1785. Early top marking. Courtesy Phillips.*
g. *1786. Top marking. Private collection.*
h. *1839. Mid-stem marking, usual in the nineteenth century to avoid damage to decoration. Courtesy Commercial Smelting Co.*
i. *1825. Bowl marking, used mostly in the nineteenth century for heavily decorated patterns. Courtesy Commercial Smelting Co.*
j. *1851. Heel marking used mostly in the nineteenth century on forks which are heavily decorated. Courtesy Commercial Smelting Co.*

What followed during the last quarter of the seventeenth century was that the marks first spread fairly evenly along the stem and then gradually grouped together at the base of the stem. The date letter moved down the stem throughout this change.

By the early eighteenth century the marks were grouped together at the base of the stem, where they remained until the end of the eighteenth century. Flatware bearing marks positioned in this way is referred to as bottom marked flatware (Figure 22).

With early Dog Nose there was little problem with the marks being struck in this

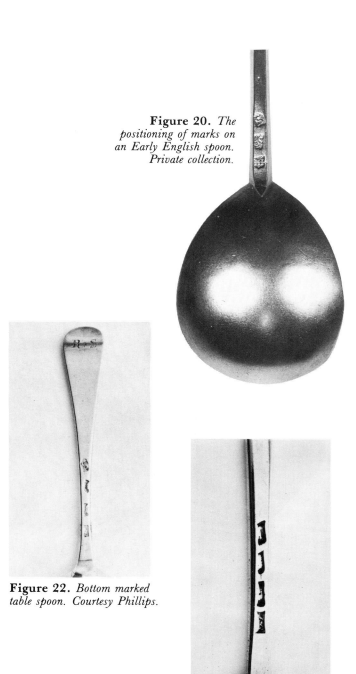

Figure 20. *The positioning of marks on an Early English spoon. Private collection.*

Figure 21. *Two slip top spoons; the child's example shows the special positioning of the date letter. Private collection.*

Figure 22. *Bottom marked table spoon. Courtesy Phillips.*

Figure 23. *Bottom marks which have been so badly distorted by reshaping the stem after hallmarking that they are very difficult to read. Courtesy Phillips.*

position since the stem was wide enough to take the punches. By about 1710, however, the bottom of the stem became much narrower and this led to an interesting problem which lasted until the marks moved to the top of the stem in the mid-1780s.

The problem was this. When the maker's mark and, subsequently, the hallmarks were stamped on the narrow part of the stem they distorted its shape by spreading the metal out sideways. After marking, the spoon maker hammered the stem back into shape. This had the effect of distorting the marks, in some cases to the point where it is completely impossible to read them (Figure 23).

To the eighteenth century spoon makers the problem lay more in the extra work involved than in the distortion of the marks, which is what concerns us today.

As will be seen from the above, the condition of a piece of flatware should never be judged by the appearance of marks (see pp. 62 and 66).

Some mid-eighteenth century spoon makers were not averse to taking advantage of this situation. What they did was quite simple and saved them both assay office charges and duty. A spoon or fork having been completed was stamped with the maker's mark only four times (Figure 24). A rare example (Figure 25) has it stamped five times. Sometimes the three makers' marks in the position of the hallmarks were stamped again, with the same punch in reverse direction, so as to make them indistinct, or a spurious punch was used. Having stamped a maker's mark and three other punches on the stem the shape of the stem was restored, making sure that the marks were closed over (Figure 26).

As it is often almost impossible to discern genuine hallmarks it is not surprising that the spoon makers generally got away with this form of duty dodging.

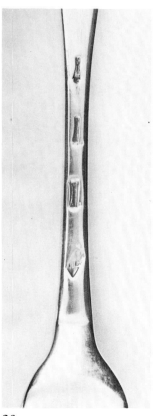

Figure 24. *Maker's mark only four times to give the impression of a set of hallmarks. George Smith c.1780. Courtesy C.J. Vander.*

Figure 25. *Maker's mark only five times. An odd example of rather overdoing it. Notice that the first punch is, as often in these cases, at a right angle to the others. Thomas and William Chawner c.1765; this particular mark was not registered at Goldsmiths' Hall. Courtesy C.J. Vander.*

Figure 26. *Maker's mark only struck once, with a spurious blank punch struck three times to resemble a set of hallmarks. Courtesy C.J. Vander.*

24   25

26

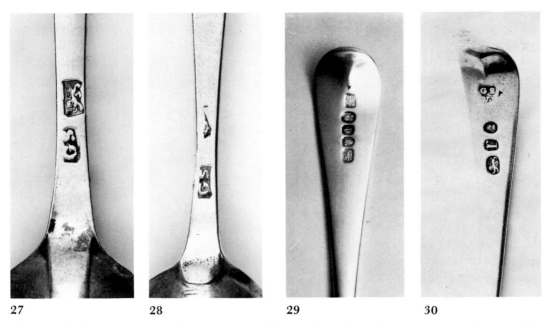

27 28 29 30

Figure 27. *Teaspoon correctly bottom marked, with maker's mark and lion passant only. Courtesy C.J. Vander.*

Figure 28. *Teaspoon bottom marked with maker's mark only struck twice, only once clearly, to resemble a correctly marked example. Courtesy C.J. Vander.*

Figure 29. *Top marked Old English pattern table spoon. Private collection.*

Figure 30. *Top marked teaspoon of the late eighteenth century correctly marked, the leopard's head omitted to prevent transposition of the marks to a larger piece. Private collection.*

The Court of Assistants required by an order of 1748 'that no spoons be assayed and tried unless they be swaged and dopt, nor no forks unless they be sawed down'. In other words spoons and forks had to be submitted in a finished state. This would make it more difficult to transpose flatware marks.

During the bottom marked period, table and dessert size flatware was normally fully marked. Teaspoons, coffee spoons, salt shovels and salt ladles were however only partially marked. Two marks are most usually found on such pieces; the correct marking was that of maker's mark and standard mark, normally the lion passant for sterling standard (Figure 27). A good many are found with the maker's mark only struck twice on the stem, once distinctly and once indistinctly (Figure 28). The reasons for this we have seen above.

The 1780s saw an important change in the positioning of the marks on spoons and forks. With the introduction of the duty mark in 1784 the marks began to be struck about three quarters of the way up the stem. This is the start of what is known as top marked flatware. By the 1790s the marks had moved slightly further up the stem, and from this period on flatware has normally been top marked (Figure 29). Top marked tea and other small spoons are usually completely marked except for the leopard's head (Figure 30). By the early nineteenth century the leopard's head is included as well.

The spoon makers must have been delighted at the lack of extra work as a result of top marking since reshaping the stem after marking was no longer necessary. The more unscrupulous amongst them must, however, have been rather upset by the new positioning now their old dodge had been thwarted by the authorities.

Makers' marks were always the first to be struck on any piece of flatware. For this reason it is the maker's mark which is found at the very base of the stem when bottom marked. When top marking began the maker's mark was again struck first but was now often at the top of the set of marks, although with top marking the mark may be found at either end of the hallmarks.

As a result of the production of more elaborate patterns in the nineteenth century it was often necessary to mark pieces in other positions to avoid damage to the decoration.

With most King's and allied patterns the marks are usually struck in the middle of the stem. More elaborate patterns sometimes had to be marked on their bowls or, with forks, in the space between the heel and the prongs.

In 1810, to curb the illegal practice of transposing (transferring) the marks from flatware to other larger pieces of silver or base metal, a special mode of marking spoons and forks was adopted.

With top marked flatware up to 1810 the hallmarks were struck horizontally so that all four could be read from left to right, each mark standing upright. The maker's mark would be at either end and at any angle to the hallmarks (Figure 31). This marking is, of course, the same as would be found on most hollow-ware.

The change that took place in London in 1810 was as follows: the four hallmarks (three after 1890) were struck so as to be read vertically with, in the case of sterling standard, the exception of the lion passant which was struck at a right angle to the others (Figures 32 and 33). This positioning of the marks from 1810 on was unique to

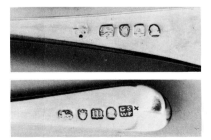

Figure 31. *Top marking before 1810 with the hallmarks stamped and each easily read from left to right. Private collection.*

Figure 32. *London flatware marks for 1840 showing the special positioning of the lion passant at a right angle to the others. Courtesy Henry Willis.*

Figure 33. *Newcastle flatware marks for 1866 showing the same special angle of the lion passant. Courtesy Sotheby's.*

flatware — should it ever be found on any other type of silver then the piece in question should be sent to the Assay Office at Goldsmiths' Hall for examination.

In 1977 this unique positioning of flatware marks was stopped, and this had the effect of saving some fifty special punches for flatware marks being cut each year. Today, therefore, flatware will be found struck with hallmarks from the same punches as other forms of silver.

Another change that took place with the introduction of top marked flatware in the eighteenth century was that all the hallmarks were struck in one operation. The maker's mark, as we have already seen, was struck individually, as it is to this day. With bottom marked flatware each of the three hallmarks was itself a separate punch. For a full set of hallmarks three separate striking operations in the Assay Office were required and the labour saved by cutting each mark into the end of one broad punch must have been quite considerable.

It is quite easy to distinguish between sets of marks which have been individually struck or struck as a group. The spacing and angles of individually struck punches are somewhat irregular. Where the marks have been struck from one punch they are far more regular, with the natural exception of the maker's mark.

The irregularity of individual stamping and the regularity of group stamping becomes more obvious with sets.

Journeymen's Marks

A journeyman was a qualified craftsman who, for various reasons, did not run his own business but worked for a master. In the large flatware-producing firms of the late eighteenth and nineteenth centuries, such as Chawner & Co., there would have been many such men.

To keep proper control on who was producing what, and to ensure that quality was maintained, each workman would have his own symbol punched on each piece he produced. These little symbols are the journeymen's marks. They are normally struck next to the maker's mark or, perhaps one should more correctly say, the mark of the firm.

The mark itself will be quite small. It may be a cross, one or more dots, a circle or perhaps a line (Figure 34). Each of these symbols would be unique to one journeyman working at one time in one firm. Similar symbols would of course be used by other firms.

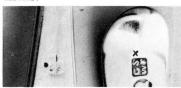

Figure 34. *Journeymen's marks stamped next to those of the firm. Private collection.*

Figure 35. *The journeyman's mark of Richard Cook. Courtesy Stuart Devlin.*

It is a fascinating exercise to examine the journeymen's marks to be found on a straight service. Quite often the spoons in such a service will be by one journeyman and the forks by another, or the table size by one and the dessert size by another.

The identification of individual journeymen from these marks has so far not been achieved and would appear to be a next to impossible task.

By the late nineteenth century the use of these marks had virtually ceased, but the idea has now been revived by Stuart Devlin and could in fact be said to have been extended. All his master craftsmen (not just the flatware makers as was the case with the original journeymen's marks) now have their own symbols which they may stamp on pieces which they have made and for which they have a special regard. The mark of Richard Cook (Figure 35) is a heart.

Odd and Rare Marks

Certain rare marks may be found on flatware.

The 'duty drawback' mark (Figure 36) used for only eight months (1st December, 1784-24th July, 1785) is a great rarity and most known examples are found on spoons.

The mark — 'Britannia standing' — was stamped on exported pieces when the duty was repaid. Although duty continued to be repaid on exported pieces after July 1785, the mark was no longer stamped since the makers complained about damage to the finish of their pieces.

'Double duty' marks can be found on silver marked in 1797 in Birmingham, Sheffield and, very rarely, Newcastle. The marking, simply the duty mark (King's head) stamped twice, resulted from the Statute of 1797 (37 Geo III, c.90) which doubled the duty on silver to 1s. per oz. (Figure 37).

Odd marking is sometimes found either as a special request from a client or because of a mistake by the worker stamping the marks in the Assay Office.

A good example of a client's special request is front marked flatware. Sets and individual examples of this rare and odd position for the marks are known from the mid-eighteenth century through to the mid-nineteenth (Figure 38).

Figure 36. *Duty drawback mark (Britannia standing). Table spoon, London, 1785, Hester Bateman. Since the letter K for 1785/6 runs from 30th May, 1785, and the duty drawback mark was used only until the 24th July of the same year, this spoon must have been marked between those two dates (i.e. only two months!). Courtesy Phillips.*

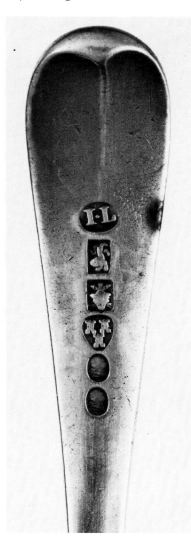

Figure 37. *Double duty marks (King's head stamped twice). A very rare Newcastle example, most are Birmingham and Sheffield. Newcastle, 1797, John Langlands. Courtesy Phillips.*

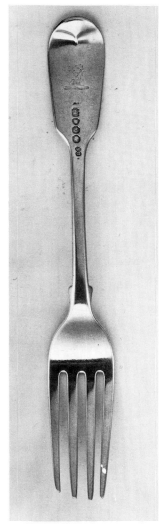

Figure 38. *Front marked fork. This unusual position for the marks would have been by the client's special request. Fiddle pattern fork, London, 1840, Benoni Stephens. Courtesy Henry Willis.*

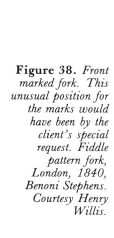

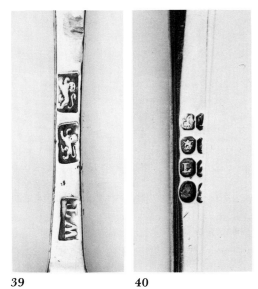

Figure 39. *Teaspoon marked by mistake with two lions passants. Courtesy C.J. Vander.*

Figure 40. *Marks badly struck and repeated. London 1806/7. Courtesy Phillips.*

39   40

Occasionally marks were stamped twice by mistake (Figure 39) or were badly struck and repeated (Figure 40).

Knives

Although not in themselves flatware, knives are so closely associated with it that a study of them and their makers is essential. The following applies equally to steel tined forks.

Haft, heft and hilt are all words which may be used for the handle of a knife. The knife handle makers were therefore described as haft, heft or hilt makers. Of the three words heft seems to have been used only rarely.

Knife Makers

Since it is not possible to get a good cutting edge on a silver blade, most knives were produced with a steel blade. The production of steel blades was quite naturally the work of a cutler, whereas that of the silver handles was that of a goldsmith or silversmith. With knives, therefore, we have a product which falls between two quite distinct trades governed by two separate livery companies, the Goldsmiths' Company and the Cutlers' Company. It is not at all surprising to find that many knife makers were freemen of the Cutlers' Company and registered marks with the Assay Office of the Goldsmiths' Company.

As we saw above with spoon makers, apprentice pedigrees reveal how closely connected many of the important haft makers were.

The Drury family are particularly interesting haft makers (see table opposite). Dru Drury, the elder, was in serious trouble with the Goldsmiths' Company in 1741. He had been involved in making a fake punch (the 'lion passant') and had been fined £100 by the Company.

In his petition which was read to the Court of Assistants on the 12th February, 1741, he said that he had been 'inadvertently concerned in causing an impression of a stamp to be made resembling the Lion Passant..., but that he hath never made any use of the stamp, and hath now caused the same to be broken; and, being sensible of his guilt, he is willing to submit himself to the Court, praying that the penalty may be moderated as the Court shall think fit.'

Apprenticeships connected with Dru Drury

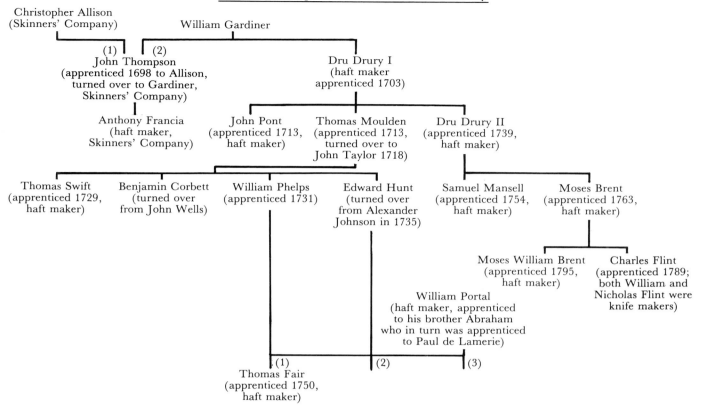

The petition was not successful and Dru Drury had to pay the full fine.

His son, also Dru, who was apprenticed to him and succeeded him as a haft maker, is in the records of the Court of Assistants for a more honourable reason. In February 1798 he wrote to the Court stating that he was 'the oldest Liveryman but one of the Goldsmiths' Company' and suggesting that during the period of the current war the money spent on livery dinners should go to the Government for the relief of financial distress. The Court debated Drury's suggestion and it was 'carried in the affirmative'.

As will be seen from the apprenticeship pedigree, a good many of the important haft makers were connected to the Drurys. In particular Moses Brent and his son Moses William Brent whose marks are found on so many late eighteenth century knives.

Another haft maker of special interest in the pedigree is Thomas Swift. In 1751, like his master's master Dru Drury, he too got into trouble with the authorities. Mr. Watson appeared before the Court of Assistants and produced written information 'against Mr. Swift, a knife-haft maker in Wood Street, for counterfeiting the Hall marks'. It was moved to 'inquire into the evidence against Thomas Swift' and to bring action if there was sufficient evidence to convict.

The haft maker Thomas Fair, as will be seen in the pedigree, had three successive masters, the first two of whom may be traced back to Dru Drury. The third, William Portal, is however of particular interest. He is listed as a haft maker in the 1773 list (see below) and had been apprenticed to his brother Abraham. Abraham had in turn been apprenticed to Lamerie who, as can be seen from his bills (pp. 34-6), included charges for fashioning knives. This would imply that knives were produced in Lamerie's workshop and not supplied by other firms. William Portal was the principal supplier of knives to Parker & Wakelin (Garrard Mss., Workmen's Ledger No. 2, Victoria and Albert Museum).

The 1773 Appendix to the Parliamentary report provides an interesting list of knife makers, two trade categories being given, that of haft maker and that of hilt maker.

Haft Makers from 1773 Parliamentary report

Workman's name	Place of abode
Abdy, William	Oat Lane, Noble Street
Aldridge, William	Red Lion Passage, Holborn
Drury, Dru	Strand
Fair, Thomas	Golden Lane
Garrard, William	Noble Street
Hirst, John	Far Field, near Sheffield, Yorkshire
Pont, John	Maiden Lane
Portal, William	Orange Street, Leicester Fields
Swift, Thomas	Old Bailey

Hilt Makers from 1773 Parliamentary report

Workman's name	Place of abode
Bennett, John	Threadneedle Street
Bock, Mark	King's Head Court, Shoe Lane
Brockus, John	Shoe Lane
Dealtrey, Thomas	Sweeting's Alley, Royal Exchange
Fayle, George	Digwell Court, White Friars
Fayle, John	No. 31, Wilderness Lane, Salisbury Court
Flint, Wm.	Dogwell Court, White Friars
Foster, Thomas	No. 16, King's Head Court, Fetter Lane
Kinman, William	East Harding Street
Lawley, Francis	Green Arbor Court
Perry, Jas.	No. 131, Chancery Lane
Radburn, John	New Street, Fetter Lane
Rawle, Wm.	Corner of Castle Court, Strand
Reynolds, John	No. 25, New Street, Fetter Lane
Thurkle, Francis	New Street, Fetter Lane

It is interesting to notice that of the eight workmen listed as haft makers working in London in 1773 (John Hirst was from Sheffield) five appear in the Dru Drury apprentice pedigree.

During the nineteenth century Sheffield occupied an increasingly dominant position in the production of knives so that today virtually all knives are produced there.

Knife Making

The construction of a knife or steel tined fork is quite different to that of a silver spoon or fork.

Having two different metals to work with (steel for the blade, or tines if a fork, and silver for the handle) presents an immediate problem. How to fix them together? The most usual solution, for all but the most modern knives, was to make the handle hollow and the blade with a tang or rod at its base which would fit into the handle. The handle would then be filled with hot pitch or shellac into which the tang of the blade would be pushed. Once cool the blade and handle would be firmly held together. Handles filled in this way are described as 'loaded'.

Hollow silver knife handles would be made in one of two ways. The best, which date mostly from the first half of the eighteenth century, were cast in two halves and soldered together. The majority were made of two halves stamped from sheet metal and then soldered together.

Modern knives differ from old ones in that the blade and handle are soldered together. This eliminates the need for a filling and thereby avoids the problems of old knives (see Pitfalls pp. 66-7). Another important difference between old and modern knives is that modern examples have rustless steel blades whereas old ones did not.

Problems (staining of the blade) have resulted from hard soldering blade and haft together. This has led to the recent adoption of sauereised handles. Here the haft is filled with a compound which is not affected by ordinary heat and, in addition, gives more weight to the haft which results in a better feel in the hand.

Fruit and dessert knives will be found from the eighteenth century to the present day with silver blades. Their construction is the same as that described above. Examples will also be found with handles of other materials such as mother-of-pearl, ivory or agate, and such knives usually have a small collar of silver, known as a ferrule, at the junction of the handle and blade.

During the late nineteenth century and on into the twentieth century many electro-plated fruit knives and forks were produced which were fitted with hallmarked silver ferrules. Since the ferrule was not soldered to the plated blade or handle this was, although deceptive, legal.

Marks on Knives

Up to the end of the eighteenth century the hafts of knives were usually only partially marked. Two marks (usually the maker's mark and one hallmark to indicate the standard) are normally found struck on the part of the haft nearest to the blade.

If the steel blades are original then they will probably be struck with a cutler's mark. If of the seventeenth or early eighteenth century the dagger mark of the Cutlers' Company will normally be found. Figures 41 and 42.

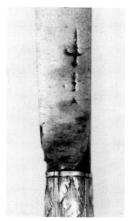

Figure 41. *Cutler's mark, a device and the dagger, c.1690/1700. Courtesy Christie's.*

Figure 42. *Cutler's mark Y and the dagger, for William Boswell (registered 1668). Courtesy Sotheby's.*

During the nineteenth century and through to the present day hafts have been fully marked. The positioning of the complete set of marks is the same as that of the earlier partial marking described above.

Where silver blades are found these may be marked in one of two ways. Either the marks will be struck on the blade itself or, more rarely, on the tang. In the case of the latter the marks are obviously not visible unless the blade has been removed from the haft.

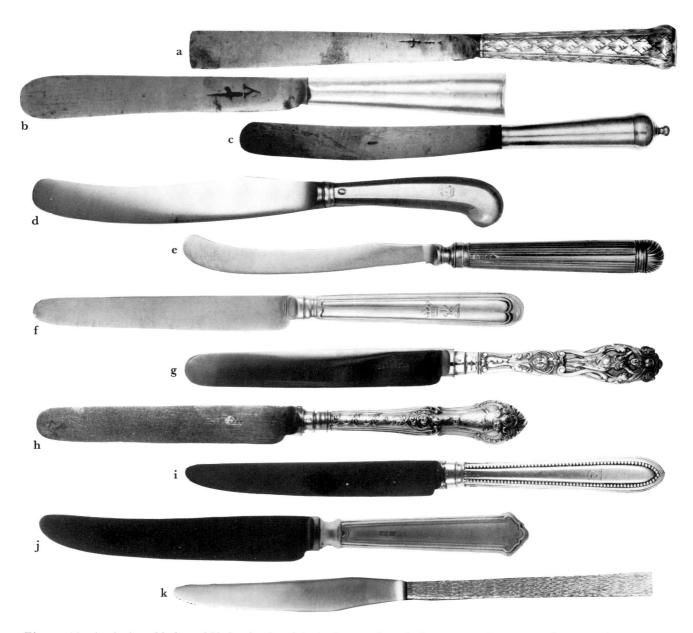

Figure 43. *A selection of hafts and blades showing their development from the late seventeenth century to the present day.*

a. *Late seventeenth century 'cannon' handle (sometimes known as seal top). Blade with spread square end. Engraved, silver gilt. The blade marked with a device and the dagger. Courtesy Christie's.*

b. *Late seventeenth century plain cylindrical handle. Blade with rounded end and marked with Y and the dagger for William Boswell (registered 1668). Courtesy Sotheby's.*

c. *Cannon handle. Blade beginning to acquire more shape, c.1700. Courtesy Sotheby's.*

d. *Pistol handle (octagonal). The blade of sabre or scimitar shape. London, c.1720. Courtesy Christie's.*

e. *Old English (Double Thread and Shell) handle. The silver blade of pronounced scimitar shape. Late eighteenth/early nineteenth century. Courtesy Sotheby's.*

f. *Old English Thread. Straight blade with slight taper and rounded end. London, 1840-41. Courtesy Sotheby's.*

g. *Rich Figure. The blade with little or no taper, rounded end. The blade shape is typical of the mid-nineteenth century. Courtesy Victoria and Albert Museum.*

h. *Pattern of unknown name. The straight blade with very slight taper, rounded end. London, 1883. Courtesy Sotheby's.*

i. *Printed Old English Bead. The blade finger point. London, 1886. Courtesy Sotheby's.*

j. *Chippendale with finger point blade. Birmingham, 1963. Courtesy Sotheby's.*

k. *Feather pattern knife by Stuart Devlin, c.1975. Courtesy Stuart Devlin.*

Knife Styles

The development of knife styles may be divided into four principal groups for the hafts, and five for the blades.

In the case of the hafts the four groups are cannon, pistol, Old English and King's and later shaped. Figure 43 shows a selection of these hafts and their development from the late seventeenth century to the present day.

The cannon (Figures 43a and c) found in the late seventeenth and early eighteenth centuries, is associated with both the Trefid and the Dog Nose patterns (see pp. 81 and 82). As the name implies the haft is shaped like a cannon, and most examples have straight-sided tapering hafts although some variants are shaped.

Pistol hafts (Figure 43d) date from the early eighteenth century through to the last quarter of that century. As with cannon the name pistol is derived from the shape of the haft.

There are many variations of the pistol — the principal ones being plain round, octagonal, strap, and shell end pistol. This pattern of haft is associated with the Hanoverian pattern (see pp. 85 and 89).

The third principal type, Old English (Figures 43e and f), was first produced to go with that flatware pattern (see pp. 95, 99, 103, 106). The end of the haft finishes straight, as with the early cannon but, unlike the cannon, which has a haft of round cross section, the Old English type has an oval cross section.

In England there was no new design of knife haft introduced for the Fiddle pattern. An interesting attempt to produce a Fiddle Thread haft may be seen in Figure 155. All the knife haft patterns which follow are decorative versions of the Old English pattern. As an example, the pattern of knife used with the Fiddle Thread and Shell pattern is in fact the Old English Thread and Shell.

In the case of the King's and later shaped patterns the haft takes its shape from the pattern.

Blades, as mentioned above, may be divided into five principal groups. These are the squared-off end, the Dutch slipper, scimitar, the finger point and the straight-rounded end.

Squared-off end blades are quite rare and found only with seventeenth century cannon handle knives (Figure 43a).

Dutch slipper and scimitar or sabre blades are the correct type to be found with pistol hafted knives. They may also be found on late cannon hafted examples (Figures 44 and 45).

Finger point blades are found with all the Old English pattern knives and its variants (Figure 43i).

Straight-rounded end blades are used extensively on various patterns in the nineteenth and early part of the twentieth century. They appear originally to have been associated mostly with ivory hafted knives and also with dessert knives (Figure 46).

Dessert knives of the late eighteenth and first half of the nineteenth century often have pointed silver blades (Figure 47).

(For details of blading see Pitfalls p. 67.)

Carvers

In addition to the straightforward table, cheese and fruit knives, carving knives and forks will be found. These were made principally in two sizes, the large size for meat and the small size for poultry. A steel for sharpening the knives will often be found with such a set.

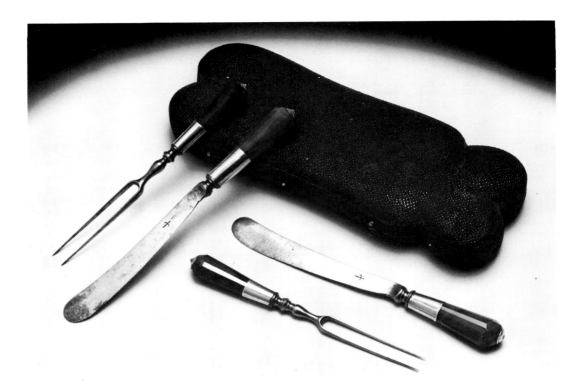

Figure 44. *Shagreen travelling case, c.1700, containing two pairs of silver mounted cornelian handled knives and forks. Marked with a heart and crown and the dagger for Ephraim How (Master of the Cutlers' Company in 1705 and working on the River Lea at Chingford). Courtesy Aspreys.*

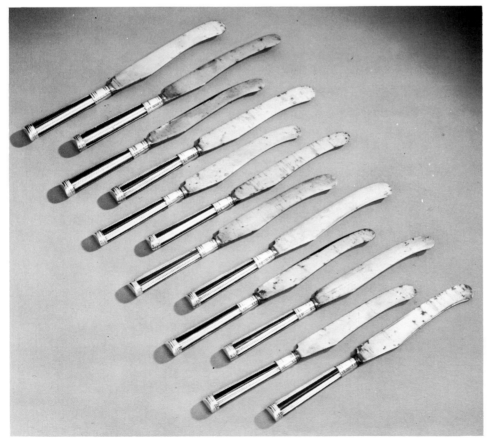

Figure 45. *Set of twelve dessert knives, c.1780, with scimitar blades and silver mounted (beaded) green stained ivory handles. Courtesy James Charles.*

Figure 46. *Fruit knife and fork with mother-of-pearl handles. Straight rounded end blade. Flat chased foliage typical of the late nineteenth/early twentieth century. Birmingham, 1891, Elkington & Co. Courtesy Sotheby's.*

Figure 47. *A selection of dessert knives.*
a. *Old English Single Thread. Pointed silver blade. London, 1801, Moses Brent. Courtesy Sotheby's.*
b. *Vine. Pointed silver blade decorated in typical Regency manner. London, 1831, William Eaton. Courtesy Sotheby's.*
c. *Nineteenth century rococo. Pointed silver blade with foliate scroll decoration typical of the mid-nineteenth century. Sheffield, 1845, Ashforth & Harthorn. Courtesy Phillips.*

English Provincial Flatware

The marks of interesting minor provincial centres may be found on seventeenth century Trefid spoons and, extremely rarely, on forks. These present a field of study and collecting in themselves as individual pieces. It would be impossible to build a service — at best collectors may specialise in a particular region, centre or maker.

The introduction of the new standard (Britannia Standard) in 1697 had a radical affect on the provincial centres. As the act was first introduced it gave no provision for any hallmarking in the provinces. It was not until 1700 that this situation was rectified by the appointment of those towns, in which mints had recently been re-established, as centres also for the hallmarking of wrought plate.

The towns appointed were York, Exeter, Bristol, Chester and Norwich. This omitted one of the most important provincial centres, Newcastle, since it had not had a mint during the recoining of the late seventeenth century. In 1702 this situation was rectified and the Newcastle Assay Office was officially established.

Later in the eighteenth century (1773) assay offices were established in both Birmingham and Sheffield.

It is important to remember that, although it may bear the marks of one of these centres, a piece may not necessarily have been made there. When the provincial centres were officially established, or re-established, at the beginning of the eighteenth century the minor centres around continued to work but now had to send their finished work to the major centre for marking.

The West Country illustrates this well as the list below shows:

Towns from which silver was sent to Exeter
for assay during the eighteenth century

Barnstaple	Liskeard
Bodmin	Modbury
Bridgwater	Penryn
Dartmouth	Plymouth
Dunster	Tiverton
Falmouth	Topsham
Fowey	Totnes
Launceston	Truro

A great deal of interest can be added to any piece by establishing where the maker was actually working. If, for example, the piece bears Exeter marks and the maker can be shown to be from Plymouth then it should be described as a Plymouth piece of silver which has been assayed in Exeter.

It should also be remembered that provincial makers would also register marks in London. The 1773 Parliamentary List of goldsmiths whose marks were entered in the Assay Office in Goldsmiths' Hall included sixty-three individuals and partnerships of all categories whose abode was outside London.

Examining each of the provincial assay offices from the early eighteenth century on we have:

Birmingham (1773 to date)

Apart from Elkington and one or two more recent manufacturers, little flatware, with the exception of caddy spoons, has ever been produced in Birmingham, but odd small pieces such as salt spoons will be found. These often have a hollow handle which is easily dented and difficult to repair.

The most interesting pieces are those produced in the eighteenth century by Matthew Boulton in his Soho works.

As far as collecting is concerned, with the exception of Elkington, Birmingham should be thought of as a source providing individual pieces of flatware only.

Bristol (eighteenth century)

Pieces bearing a Bristol mark are of the utmost rarity, and only a handful of pieces are known. This centre is mainly of academic interest. Look out for London or Exeter marked pieces by Bristol makers.

Chester (1701-1962)

Odd pieces of flatware may be found.

In the late nineteenth and early twentieth centuries silver was sent from Birmingham to be marked in Chester. Sets of late nineteeth and twentieth century coffee and teaspoons bearing Chester marks will most often be from Birmingham.

The collecting of Chester marked flatware is best confined to individual pieces; the building of sets would be virtually impossible.

Exeter (1701-1882)

A good amount of Exeter flatware may be found mostly of the Old English and the Fiddle pattern; the Fiddle pattern, in particular, being produced in large quantities during the first half of the nineteenth century.

Services of Exeter flatware may be found. Should you wish to build a Fiddle pattern service then Exeter marked should be considered. When building a service Exeter flatware should not be mixed with London.

Newcastle (1702-1883)

A good amount of Newcastle flatware survives in services, sets and as individual pieces.

The Fiddle and Shell pattern appears to have been particularly popular here in the nineteenth century, and as much will be found with Newcastle marks as with London.

If the Fiddle or Fiddle and Shell patterns are chosen then building a Newcastle service would be possible.

Norwich (c.1701)

Of academic interest only, eighteenth century Norwich silver being of the utmost rarity.

Sheffield (1773 to date)

Eighteenth and early nineteenth century Sheffield flatware is quite scarce. From the mid-nineteenth century on, with the development of machine-made flatware, vast quantities have been produced in this centre.

Although in the eighteenth century and early nineteenth century a good many haft makers (see p. 48) worked in London, by the end of the nineteenth century Sheffield had almost completely taken over. Today virtually all knives are made in Sheffield.

Large numbers of late nineteenth and twentieth century services of different patterns may be found. Building a service is possible but not as easy as might at first be thought, since most services are still intact.

Always bear in mind with Sheffield flatware that it will, with only very rare exceptions, be machine made (see pp. 22 and 24).

York (1701-1713, 1778-1856)

No York silver has been recorded between 1713 and 1778. The Assay Office was closed in 1717 and did not reopen until after 1773.

Flatware of the late eighteenth and first half of the nineteenth century is scarce but can be found.

Services of York flatware are known to exist including one of the rare Old English Thread and Shell pattern. Building a service of Old English or Fiddle pattern would be extremely difficult but possible over a long period of time.

York often omitted to stamp its pieces with the town mark and the resulting set of marks can be mistaken for London, although the character of the individual punches is quite different. The York crowned leopard's head, in particular, is usually in a rectangular punch.

Irish Flatware

The majority of what has already been said about English flatware may be applied to Irish flatware.

It is consistently of a fine heavy quality; often, indeed, better than a good many of the pieces made in England. However, although the pieces were mostly made to a very high standard, they were often not treated with quite the same respect as their English counterparts. The wear on some Irish pieces is quite phenomenal.

Style

The greatest achievement of the Irish goldsmiths producing flatware was without doubt their bright-cut patterns of the late eighteenth and early nineteenth centuries.

The most popular was the Star design which was produced mostly in Dublin. The other three which may be found are the Bow, which was also from Dublin, as was the rare Rose. The very rare Plumes is found mostly from Limerick. In each case the motif appears at the top of the stem.

Rare combinations may also be found, such as Bow and Star bright-cut, or Fiddle pattern with Plumes bright-cut (Figure 48), but such pieces are so rare that building a service would be impossible.

The Old English pattern in Ireland was given a pointed instead of a rounded end; as a result of this the full description of particular patterns does start to become rather lengthy. For example, in plain form it is Irish pointed Old English, but with Star bright-cutting it becomes Irish pointed Old English Star bright-cut. This does get a bit tedious and, as a result, expressions such as Irish Star or Irish Bow pattern are used.

During the nineteenth and twentieth centuries copies of these Irish bright-cut patterns were produced in England and in recent years the practice of bright-cut engraving plain eighteenth and early nineteenth century Irish pieces has increased alarmingly. This applies particularly to forks which are rare to find with original bright-cutting.

Although most Irish patterns lag a few years behind their English counterparts surprises are to be found. Amongst the earliest recorded examples of Fiddle pattern from anywhere in the British Isles is a pair of Dublin gravy spoons dated 1758, and a set of table spoons and forks of the same year (Figure 49).

A variation which appears to be peculiar to Ireland, is turned-over or hook-end flatware. This is found principally with eighteenth century serving pieces. As the name implies, the end of the stem is literally turned back for hanging the piece up (Figure 50).

Another unusual feature in Ireland is the appearance, in the early nineteenth century, of the rat tail on the newly popular Fiddle pattern. With Irish Fiddle pattern it is therefore necessary to distinguish between Fiddle with rat tail and Fiddle without rat tail (Figure 51).

Figure 48. *Irish Fiddle with Plumes bright-cut. A rare combination. Teaspoon, Limerick, c.1800, Robert O'Shaughnessy. Courtesy Phillips.*

Figure 49. *Early Irish Fiddle pattern. Part of a set of twenty-four each of table spoons and forks. Notice the unusual feature of a rococo decorated top and the lack of shoulders. Dublin, 1758, Thomas Williamson. Courtesy Christie's.*

Figure 50. *Irish turned-over or hook-end flatware. Dublin, 1761. Courtesy Phillips.*

Figure 51. *Irish Fiddle with rat tail. Pair of sauce ladles, Dublin, 1828, Charles Marsh. Courtesy M. McAleer.*

Marks

Among collectors of Irish silver those who specialise in flatware are particularly fortunate as regards hallmarks.

During the eighteenth century a somewhat unusual system of marking objects was adopted in Ireland in that, for the most part, large pieces were only partially marked. If the maker's mark was struck then the date letter was omitted and vice versa. Flatware, however, was mostly completely and painstakingly hallmarked. The exceptions here are mostly the very small pieces such as tea, salt and mustard spoons.

A mistake frequently made is to confuse Irish marks, particularly if worn, with Britannia Standard English marks. The appearance of a crowned harp (Irish) or leopard's head erased (English) should eliminate any possiblity of confusion. Should, however, only the figure of Britannia or of Hibernia be visible then always remember that Hibernia rests her arm on a harp.

Irish Provincial

The two principal centres from which flatware may be found, are Cork and Limerick, the vast majority coming from Cork although even these are by no means plentiful.

Quite a range of patterns are known from Cork including some quite rare ones such as Onslow.

On the other hand, Limerick flatware, though much more limited in range, does include the rare bright-cut Plumes, all the known pieces of which, with rare Dublin exceptions, are from this centre.

Other provincial centres such as Galway, Kinsale and Youghal occur so rarely as to be mostly of academic interest.

For the most part the collecting of Irish provincial flatware has to be confined to individual pieces of various designs, dates and makers, and consequently the building of a service would be virtually impossible.

Scottish Flatware

Generally speaking what has already been said on the subject of English flatware applies equally to Scottish.

Style

The market for silver as a whole in Scotland was a smaller and mostly less wealthy one than that in England, and as a result two important differences evolved, both of which are most apparent in the nineteenth century.

First the range of patterns was much more limited — it is quite rare to find any but the most usual of patterns from Scotland.

Secondly, when decorative patterns such as King's and Queen's were produced the Scots were not inclined to have decoration where it was not going to be seen. As a result the top surface was normally the only one to receive any decoration. This is referred to as single struck flatware, i.e. the decoration is struck on one side only.

It is usual, therefore, when referring to pieces decorated in this way, to talk of, for example, Scottish single struck King's pattern.

Scottish double struck pieces, i.e. with decoration on both surfaces, are sometimes found but these are quite scarce.

The decoration itself is usually a simplified version of the English form. This is best illustrated by comparing the lower stem sections of Scottish and English King's pattern; the former is usually quite plain (known as single struck half King's), whereas with the English the thread edge continues to the base of the stem.

Most patterns from the late eighteenth century onwards are noticeably lighter than their English counterparts.

Scottish Old English pattern is often finished with a more pointed end than is usual in England (see also Irish pointed Old English, p. 56).

A word should be said about the Fiddle pattern in Scotland. There are, in effect, two different styles which may be referred to as Fiddle and to save any confusion it is best to qualify the use of the word Fiddle by the addition of the words 'English type', or 'Scottish type'. English Fiddle is discussed below (see pp. 108 and 109). An example of this pattern which is found bearing Scottish marks should be described as Scottish Fiddle pattern of English type. The proportions of Scottish Fiddle of English type are often different to English examples (see Figure 140).

Scottish Fiddle is found mostly in the middle and later years of the eighteenth century. The end of the stem spreads out more gradually than English Fiddle and is waisted, unlike the English type. Another important difference is that the end of the stem turns up in Hanoverian manner and is often ribbed. Most examples to be found are teaspoons (see p. 88).

Teaspoons with unusually long stems are found with Scottish marks. These are generally described as teapot or mash spoons and were used for stirring the pot and appear to be peculiar to Scotland (see p. 207).

Scottish teaspoons are found with numbers engraved on them. This appears to have been a practice for making identification easier at tea parties.

As regards engraving it is useful to remember that when a crest and motto was displayed in Scotland the motto was put in a semicircle above the crest. In England the motto was put below the crest. This can be a particularly good guide to a Scottish origin if a piece is otherwise partially or badly marked.

Scottish Provincial

The majority of surviving Scottish provincial silver is flatware and the majority of that is spoons, particularly teaspoons. Most examples will be in a plain pattern — Hanoverian, Old English or Fiddle (both Scottish and English), depending on period.

Lists of the Scottish provincial town marks are readily available. However, a point that should be remembered, is that a number of Scottish goldsmiths worked in India in the late eighteenth and nineteenth centuries, and the marks which they struck on their pieces were frequently based on those of their home town. Flatware will therefore be found with what appear to be Scottish provincial marks but which in fact are those of Scottish goldsmiths working in the Indian sub-Continent.

Old Sheffield Plate

Examples of old Sheffield plate flatware other than sugar tongs, caddy spoons and teaspoons are rare. This was one of the few areas in which both the eighteenth and nineteenth century manufacturers failed, basically for two reasons. First, the assembled parts were not strong enough for the rigorous use to which flatware may be put. Secondly, once copper was exposed verdigris would form; this is poisonous and continued use of such a piece would be dangerous.

When found, spoons have their bowls and stems soldered together, while the stems are often made of two stamped halves soldered along their length.

Forks are extremely rare. When found the tops of the prongs are usually of silver.

Serving pieces such as soup ladles and gravy spoons are occasionally found (Figures 52 and 53).

Old Sheffield knife hafts are rare but can also be found (Figure 54).

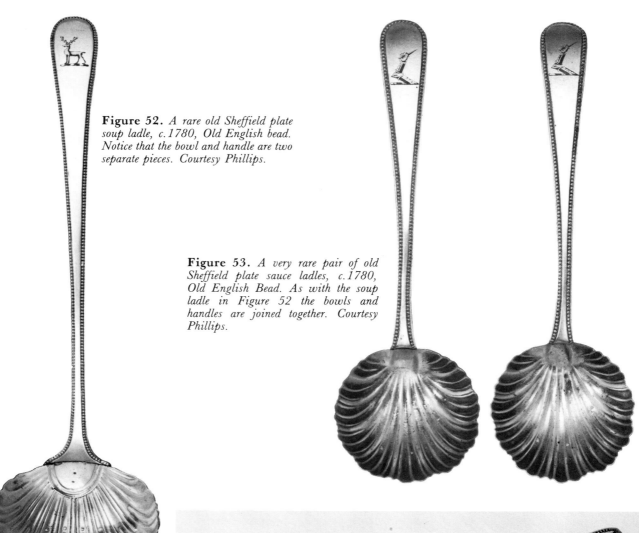

Figure 52. *A rare old Sheffield plate soup ladle, c.1780, Old English bead. Notice that the bowl and handle are two separate pieces. Courtesy Phillips.*

Figure 53. *A very rare pair of old Sheffield plate sauce ladles, c.1780, Old English Bead. As with the soup ladle in Figure 52 the bowls and handles are joined together. Courtesy Phillips.*

Figure 54. *A delightful old Sheffield plate fish slice, c.1780, Old English Pointed Bead. It is a rare example of hand-pierced old Sheffield plate. Courtesy Phillips.*

Close Plate

Close plated flatware is found much more frequently than old Sheffield plate. The base metal in this case is iron or steel, the silver being attached to the surface with tin (under heat).

Most pieces found will be fruit and dessert knives and forks although there is a good amount of table flatware (Figure 55). Fiddle pattern of the nineteenth century predominates among the surviving examples.

Should you be in any doubt that a piece is close plated, then test it with a magnet, which should stick to it.

One of the disadvantages of this type of flatware is that if the metal is rusted or the piece damaged in any way, it cannot be repaired.

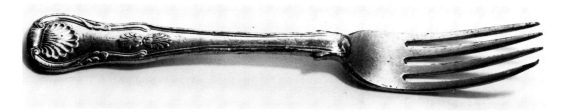

Figure 55. *A close plate fork. Private collection.*

Figure 56. *Close plate mark 'Silk'. It was usual for a close plater to use his full name. Private collection.*

Electro-Plate

From the mid-nineteenth century to the present day vast quantities of electro-plated flatware of every conceivable pattern have been produced.

Many of the marks stamped on these pieces, particularly up to the end of the nineteenth century, resemble, at a glance, silver marks, but a close examination should show immediately that the individual punches only vaguely resemble true silver marks. The feel of electro-plated flatware is also quite different from silver being much harder and colder.

Should you contemplate purchasing electro-plated flatware, remember that second-hand it has little value, and virtually none if the base metal is worn through, the reason for this being that it costs almost as much to replate a service as it does to make a new one. A replated service will rarely have a good surface.

At present, and as far as can be seen in the future, electro-plated flatware, unless by a special designer such as Dresser or Mackintosh (see pp. 155 and 157), has no investment potential at all.

See Figure 57.

Figure 57. *Elkington sample electro-plated table forks and a spoon. Notice that the marks give a visual impression of a set of hallmarks being stamped in the same position and having a similar number of marks. Courtesy C.J. Vander.*

Pitfalls

Condition

Of all the factors which should be taken into account when assessing any genuine piece, set or service, condition is the most important.

How then may condition be judged? Perhaps the first point that should be made is that a piece of flatware should never be judged on hallmarks. Marks may be weakly struck, mis-struck or, as has been discussed above with bottom marking (pp.40-1), be distorted in the process of manufacture. Unless you are collecting marks and not flatware their condition is misleading and of only secondary importance.

How to Judge Spoon Condition

The quickest, and normally safest, way of judging the condition of a spoon is to examine the edges of the bowl.

When a spoon is new it has a flat edge running round the bowl which varies in width, the narrowest parts being the sides and back of the bowl, the broadest being at the front (Figure 58a). It is not possible to give specific measurements for these edges since they will vary with the quality and maker of any given spoon.

Once in use these edges start to wear away, although the wear is not even over the whole of the spoon edge. The front and front left- or right-hand sides naturally receive the most wear, and it is for this reason that the front edge is the thickest. Eventually, while the sides retain their original thickness the front will be worn to a knife edge (Figure 58b).

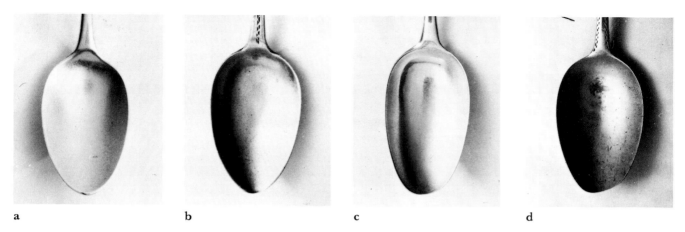

a   b   c   d

Figure 58. *Progressive wear of spoon bowls. Courtesy Phillips.*

At this point the bowl still retains its original shape, but subsequently the sharp front edge starts to curl back (it is possible to catch this with a thumb nail and make a clicking noise) (Figure 58c), and from this point on the bowl starts losing its shape and the spoon will shortly be fit only for scrap (Figure 58d). (See also Reshaped Spoon Bowls p. 65.)

How to Judge Fork Condition

The tips of the prongs or tines are the best indication of wear. When new, all three or four prongs will be the same length; as the fork is used so the prongs wear down at an uneven rate, the side prongs wearing faster than the central prong or prongs (Figure 59).

Figure 59. *A typical example of badly worn tines. Courtesy Henry Willis.*

Look also at the backs of the prongs to see how badly cut they are — cuts resulting from their being used with steel knives.

Forks will quite often have their prongs trimmed when they become uneven through wear. Look at the proportions of the prongs — do they balance well with the rest of the fork? A very small amount of trimming is acceptable, especially if the prongs were particularly long. In some cases, however, forks are found with ridiculously stubby prongs which are quite out of proportion with the rest of the fork (Figure 60).

Condition of Handles or Stems

For the most part the handles of spoons and forks do not suffer from signs of wear to the same extent as do bowls and prongs.

In the case of plain patterns the most obvious signs will be worn crests or initials. Judging condition on any engraving is dangerous unless it can be shown to be original (see Engraving, p. 66). Decorative patterns which have die-stamped decoration, such as the King's or Queen's patterns, are easier to judge. Look at the high points of the decoration to see how sharp it is. The best place to examine is the point of contact with the table when the spoon or fork is put down since this naturally gets the hardest wear (Figure 60).

Solder Joins

With only rare exceptions such as the Onslow pattern (see p. 172), there should never be any solder join whatsoever on any part of any spoon or fork.

Solder will show as a discoloration on the surface and is always much easier to see if you breathe over the piece. In most cases such solder joins as are found will be quite honest repairs where stems, bowls, or prongs have split.

60

61

62

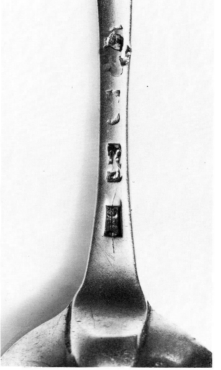

Figure 60. *On the left a fork in very fine condition; on the right a badly worn example with a regimental crest which has had its tines trimmed; it is not very old and typical of the rather hard use which regiments gave their flatware. Courtesy C.J. Vander.*

Figure 61. *Typical repair to a split stem. Notice that the soldered split has occurred where the date letter has been stamped, and that another fracture of the metal runs the length of the stem through the maker's mark. With bottom marking it is not unusual to find one or other of these faults. Courtesy M. McAleer.*

Figure 62. *Repaired (soldered) split in the bowl of a spoon (dessert size) near its junction with the stem. Courtesy M. McAleer.*

The point which should be particularly examined for signs of solder is, with a spoon or fork, the lower half of the stem. This is the most likely place for it to split, particularly if bottom marked. Look all round the stem and, if bottom marked, at each of the marks (Figure 61).

Spoon bowls tend to split mostly at each side of the junction of bowl with stem. Repairs in this area often leave a white 'stain' at the back of the bowl (Figure 62). The whole of a spoon bowl should be examined for solder lines running across where worn bowls have been either completely or partially replaced.

Forks should be examined carefully at the base of the prongs and along the length of each prong. Any three-prong fork (Trefid, Dog Nose or Hanoverian) must be most carefully examined. They are amongst the most faked of all objects in English silver. The most common method of faking is to cut off the bowl of a spoon and replace it by soldering on 'prongs', and when this has been done the solder join will most usually appear at the base of the stem below the hallmarks (Figure 66). Natural splits generally occur amongst the hallmarks which tend to create a weak point in the stem. (See also Cast Fakes and Altered Pieces, pp. 67-70.)

Solder joins are sometimes covered by electro-plating the repaired spoon or fork.

Reshaped Spoon Bowls

Worn spoon bowl fronts are often 'restored' by stretching the existing metal of the bowl and, when done properly to a bowl front which has just started to curl back, this can extend the life of a spoon.

The signs to look for are hammer marks on the front underside of the bowl which do not match the rest of the bowl.

Many spoons will be found where this type of 'restoration' has been taken to extremes. The bowls in such cases are very thin, very whippy, and usually quite out of shape. Such spoons are only fit for scrap.

Stretched Fork Prongs

In order to increase the length of the prongs on a worn fork the metal is sometimes stretched by hammering. Such forks should be avoided since the prongs will not be strong enough for normal use. It is better to have honest, strong but perhaps slightly short fork prongs than to have stretched examples. For an indication of this type of 'restoration' look for hammer marks on the prongs, and feel how strong they are.

Electro-Plating

Silver flatware is sometimes electro-plated, i.e. placed in a vat of silver salts through which a current flows in such a way that the object placed in the vat is covered with pure silver.

There are three principal reasons why this is done. The first and most common is to cover solder joins where they are not supposed to be. The second is to add weight and substance to an otherwise light service. The third is to cover the stain where a crest has been removed (see p. 66).

When a piece, or service, has been electro-plated it will have a whiter than normal surface since pure silver only is deposited. If the stem is carefully examined, it is possible to see the point at which the wire holding the piece in the vat was in contact with the stem. It will appear as a slight depression running round the stem, usually at an angle. If you suspend a spoon or fork by a loosely-tied piece of string you will see the sort of line such a mark will make.

Other indications of electro-plating, especially if heavy, will be a slight blurring of the marks or of any engravings, although this can, of course, occur for other reasons.

If the proper facilities and skills are available, then subjecting silver flatware to the fire will remove the plate and reveal the truth.

Chemical tests of the surface silver will reveal whether the piece has been electro-plated or not. Both sterling and Britannia standard silver are alloys containing copper. Silver can only be deposited in a pure state by electro-plating.

Any piece, set or service of silver flatware which has been electro-plated should be avoided.

Engraving

The majority of flatware has at some time in its life been engraved with some form of identification, mostly crests or initials. Many pieces have also had their engraving replaced or simply removed at some time. How then is it possible to tell whether any engraving is original or not, or, indeed, if engraving has been erased?

The style of the engraving is of great importance. Script initials with foliate embellishments (mid-eighteenth century) would obviously have been engraved at a later date if found on a Queen Anne piece, as would the conjoined initials of the late nineteenth century on a George III piece.

The greatest problem arises when a piece is engraved in the correct style but at a later period or, for that matter, when an original engraving is touched up.

Perhaps the best initial test is simply to compare the sharpness of engraving with the overall condition of the piece. Worn or restored spoon bowls or fork prongs with sharp engraving tell their own story. Should a piece have passed the above test then look around any engraving for traces of an earlier one. Odd sections of particularly deep engraving are not easy to get rid of. Then look at the end of the stem at a glancing angle to the light and turn it from side to side. The appearance of a slight hollow at this point will indicate the removal of an earlier engraving by filing and stoning it away.

There are two other ways in which engravings have been, and are, removed.

One is an extension of the most usual method (filing), where the stem is hammered behind the engraving in order to force the metal forward and thus eliminate the hollow. When this is done hammer marks can usually be seen on the back of the stem.

The other is to fill the engraving with solder and then smooth the surface down. This will leave a stain which can sometimes be seen. However, most such pieces are then electro-plated over to cover this stain.

Re-engraving and erasures are certainly not modern phenomena; the re-engraving and removal of crests and initials was carried out regularly by the goldsmiths of the past. There are mixed views on the matter and pieces should be taken on their merit — a well erased piece in good condition is certainly more desirable than a worn out one with an original crest.

The most serious drawback to erasure, even when done well, is that it spoils the patina at the top of the stem. Where present it will also cut through the grey fire skin exposing the whiter silver below.

Knife Condition

All knife hafts must be most carefully examined for splits, repairs, and even missing pieces of silver. The problem with all old knives is that if the haft gets hot the filling melts and expands. If you are lucky this will simply push the blade out; if not, then the haft will split and require soldering. Over the years many hafts have been repaired several times and are today only fit for scrap.

The most usual cause of hafts getting hot is through their being immersed in washing-up water. When washing an old knife always hold the haft out of the water —

never immerse it. Direct sunlight on knife hafts has also been known to cause similar damage.

Hafts should also be examined for cuts which result from knives being put together in a drawer or when a table is cleared. They should always be stored, and handled, in such a way that the steel blades will not come into contact with the silver hafts.

Knife blades have often been replaced. If this has been done in the correct style such replacements may be quite acceptable; if not, then the knife will probably look decidedly odd.

Old blades are always a problem to keep in good condition since they will rust and stain easily. However, they do have a much better cutting edge than modern ones and this should be remembered when cleaning.

Should reblading be necessary, as it often is, then make sure that the new blades are of the correct style, that they have a dull (butler) surface, and that no names, etc. appear on the blade.

Victorian and twentieth century electro-plated hafts with hallmarked silver ferrules are a trap for the unwary. Such ferrules should not be soldered to the electro-plated hafts.

Fakes, Forgeries and Alterations

Flatware fakes may be put into two categories: the outright fake, where no part of the piece is original; and the alteration, where part of the piece may be original but is so altered that its character is changed.

The penalties for forging hallmarks or transposing them from one piece to another are, and always have been, severe, and anybody convicted of such an offence today is liable to a prison sentence of up to ten years. It is also possible to be prosecuted for possession of a forged or illegally altered piece. Should you ever suspect that a piece of flatware in your possession fits into one of these categories then the authorities at one of the assay offices should be consulted.

Cast Fakes

These are found mostly with early patterns such as Trefid and Dog Nose, together with three-prong forks, and pieces with famous makers' marks.

When found in sets detection is easy; all the marks are struck, or mis-struck, in exactly the same position and manner (Figures 63 and 64) on each piece of the same type (i.e. table spoons, dessert forks, etc.). On genuine pieces the marks were struck individually by hand and it would, therefore, be quite impossible for the marks to be exactly the same.

With late eighteenth century and later marks it should be remembered that the hallmarks were struck together, but that the maker's marks were struck separately. There will, therefore, be a variation in the spacing and angle of the hallmarks to the maker's marks. The hallmarks themselves, with this later type of marking, will vary as a group with their positioning on the stem of each piece. They will also vary slightly in strength of punch although such variation is found mostly with maker's marks.

The above points make it easy to detect cast fakes when found in sets. When found as individuals detection is more difficult.

Probably the best method of testing is to carry out a similar test to that discussed above for distinguishing between hand- and machine-made pieces (see p. 22).

Cast metal is quite different in structure from the metal in hand- or machine-made pieces. It is quite rigid; therefore, when any attempt is made to test the stem or bowl, there is absolutely no give at all.

Figure 63. *Set of three cast forgeries of Trefid table spoons. Notice that each punch is stamped in exactly the same position and manner on each spoon. These have been cast from a genuine example of 1698. Compare them with a genuine set (Figure 3). Courtesy Goldsmiths' Hall.*

Figure 64. *Set of six cast forgeries of Trefid condiment spoons. As with Figure 63 all the punches are identical. It would be very surprising to find a set of condiment spoons at this date (1698 according to the date letter). Courtesy Phillips.*

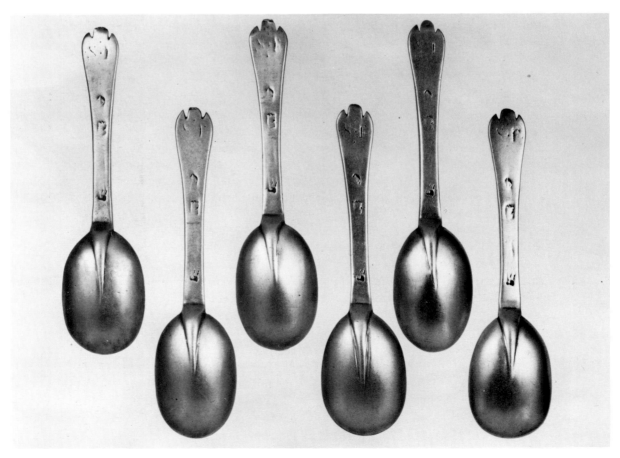

Other indications may be a rather granular appearance to the marks or a slight pitting over the surface due to oxygen bubbling out of the molten silver while cooling (pitting, though, can also result from burial).

Altered Pieces

The greatest danger here is with three-prong forks. Some people go so far as to say that any eighteenth century three-prong fork should be regarded as a probable fake until it can be proved to be genuine. It is certainly the safest approach. The conversion of spoon to three-prong fork by replacing the spoon bowl has already been covered above (p. 65); see also Figures 65 and 66.

There is a much more dangerous type of conversion which is carried out without the removal of the bowl. With this conversion the bowl is first hammered flat. The sides are then turned in to produce the shape and thickness of the end of a fork, new metal being added in any gaps if necessary. Solder is then flushed over the end. When this has been completed the prongs are cut and the fake three-prong fork is ready.

Detection of such a conversion is more difficult than the other two methods (casting and replacing). Three-prong forks, with both replaced and converted bowls, are often detected initially by their generally bad proportions. Converted bowls may also be detected by examining the prongs for solder joins running along the inside edges. Look also for signs of removed rat tails, etc.

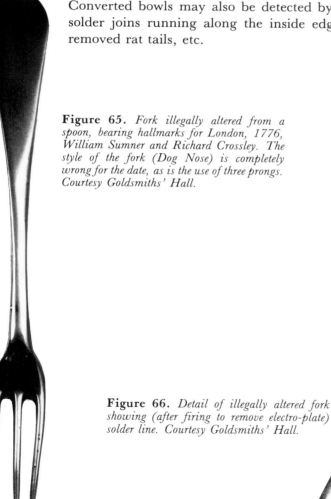

Figure 65. *Fork illegally altered from a spoon, bearing hallmarks for London, 1776, William Sumner and Richard Crossley. The style of the fork (Dog Nose) is completely wrong for the date, as is the use of three prongs. Courtesy Goldsmiths' Hall.*

Figure 66. *Detail of illegally altered fork showing (after firing to remove electro-plate) solder line. Courtesy Goldsmiths' Hall.*

Figure 67. *Fake apostle and seal top spoons made by reshaping eighteenth century table spoons and adding the cast finials. Courtesy Phillips.*

Figure 68. *Three original apostle spoons for comparison with those in Figure 67. Private collection.*

Another danger is the fairly plentiful supply of apostle and other early English types of spoon found with eighteenth century marks. All of these, virtually without exception, are converted from eighteenth century table spoons. Once aware of this fact there should be no chance of falling into the trap (Figure 67).

Gilding

Since the majority of flatware was not gilded, all gilded pieces must be carefully examined. Covering the surface of silver with a layer of gold has always been one of the best ways of covering the stain of solder joins where they should not be. Always look very carefully at the points discussed above (pp. 64 and 65) for irregularities in the surface.

Later Decoration (see also Engraving above)

During the mid-nineteenth century the practice of producing 'berry' spoons started.

The bowls and stems of earlier plain spoons were embossed and chased with fruit and foliate scrolls, mostly on table spoons of the Hanoverian and Old English patterns although no pattern or size was safe. Seventeenth century Trefid spoons were not ignored by the hands of later decorators, neither were salt spoons, basting spoons nor, for that matter, forks.

Later engraved decoration is not found as frequently as chasing, since it was a more expensive process.

Any piece of flatware bearing marks of a date prior to the mid-nineteenth century which has decoration similar to those pieces illustrated (Figures 69 and 70) will have been later decorated. It is quite wrong for example to talk of a 'George III, Old English pattern berry spoon' — they simply were not made.

The only way such a piece may properly be described is as a George III Old English pattern spoon with later decoration. Sad to say, such is the popularity of these mongrel pieces, that this base practice continues today.

Fire Stain or Skin

Fire stain results from the oxidation of copper in the alloy of both sterling and Britannia standard silver during the repeated annealings when made by hand.

It gives a grey blue surface to any piece where it occurs and is one of the principal reasons for the colour people associate with old silver. With use and polishing this surface skin wears away to reveal the whiter colour of the silver below. This can give the surface a motley or stained appearance.

Flatware of the seventeenth and eighteenth centuries should, if in good condition, have an intact fire skin. Repairs and the removal of engravings will damage this skin, which can never be simulated, leaving white patches.

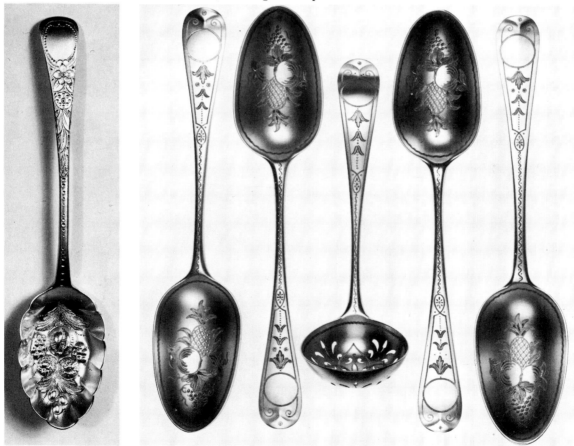

69 **Figure 69.** *A George III plain Old English pattern table spoon which has been decorated 'berry' style in the mid-nineteenth century. Private collection.* **70**

Figure 70. *Later decorated mid-eighteenth century flatware. Originally plain, these have been engraved and then gilded with a pearl finish. The sifter spoon was pierced at the same time — it was originally a sauce ladle. Courtesy Sotheby's.*

Bastards

The term 'bastard' has been, and still is, used to describe any oddity. There are three principal areas in which it may be applied: size, pattern and mixture of dies. Most, if not all such pieces, result from special orders.

Size: any piece of any odd size.

Pattern: odd variants of standard patterns (see 'Scottish Bastard King's' p. 123).

Mixture of dies: these are often produced from half dies (see p. 25) and can be any combination of dies of the correct size.

Pitfalls with Specific Patterns

These have been given where necessary in the section on each pattern in Part II.

Building a Service

This refers to the practice of acquiring a flatware service piece by piece over a period of time rather than purchasing a complete service.

Building a service can either be a very enjoyable and rewarding pursuit or highly frustrating. Which depends very much on how you begin.

Having decided to build a service, various factors must be taken into account to ensure both enjoyment and success.

First, it is important that you choose a style which you are going to enjoy using and which will fit happily with your existing or planned dining equipment. Having decided upon this you should then make sure that the pattern chosen is within your price range.

Another important point to bear in mind is the availability of the pattern as a whole. Some patterns, such as the Bacchanalian (pp. 127-8), were only originally produced for dessert services; this is fine if that is what you require, but highly frustrating to discover having embarked on building a complete service.

If your chosen pattern has failed one of the above requirements then try to find either a similar one which will pass, or perhaps a later version of it.

Having established the required pattern, the next stage depends on how close you wish the individual pieces in your final service to be in date. If you are not worried about a wide range of dates and makers then any of the pieces can be acquired as soon as they are found.

If, however, you aim to build a service with a close range of dates or with all pieces by the same maker, then another approach must be taken.

The best approach in either case is to purchase the dessert forks first and then match the rest of the service to them. It is much easier to match table size pieces to the dessert pieces than vice versa.

Should you intend to build a service by the same maker then choose an available one such as one made by the Eley, Fearn and Chawner partnerships.

Slight fluctuation of size and detail in design will be most apparent when the pieces in a service are put together. Remember, however, that when the pieces are placed round a table such variations will not be apparent and, anyway, you may not mind if they are only slight.

Acquiring a Complete Service

Each service, whether straight or mixed, must, of course, be judged on its merits. Condition is of prime importance and, after that, in the case of a mixed service, how good a mix it is.

Should you wish to purchase a straight service then the following points should be considered. If a piece is lost from a service it will be very difficult to find a replacement of the same pattern, maker and year, and almost impossible if the service is of an obscure pattern.

Another consideration with a service of obscure pattern is that should you wish to increase the size of the service in the future it may not be possible.

Values

Pieces in exceptionally fine condition will command a premium above the norm; examples in poor condition will be worth less; and, if in really poor condition, unless exceptionally rare, then the current price of scrap silver will give the value.

Important makers such as Paul de Lamerie or Paul Storr will always double or treble the value as will fashionable makers such as Hester Bateman.

Value can also be increased by the appearance of crests, etc., identifying pieces with important past owners such as, for example, members of the royal family, Byron or Nelson. With any such crest always make certain that it is original. The practice of 'improving' pieces by engraving them with the heraldic devices of famous people is not unknown.

One would expect rare nineteenth century patterns to be more expensive than standard examples, but the reverse is, in fact, normally the case, since they are difficult to build into services.

Part 2

The Patterns

These are grouped according to principal type (e.g. Old English Feather Edge under Old English; King's Husk under King's Shape, etc.). The principal pattern types are arranged as follows:

Trefid

Dog Nose

Hanoverian

Old English

Fiddle

King's Shape

Mid- and Late Nineteenth Century

Arts and Crafts, Aesthetic Movement, Art Nouveau and Allied Patterns

Twentieth Century, 1900-1950

Twentieth Century, 1950-1980

Other Patterns

Serving Pieces

Miscellaneous Pieces

Trefid

The Trefid pattern was the first to be produced in services and thus starts the history of flatware patterns in England. The earliest English examples date from about 1660 and derive from the Puritan spoon. The name, Trefid, results from the spread at the top of the stem which is divided into three by two notches cut into the end.

One of the most useful developments in shape which assists in dating is the evolution of stem shape. Early examples (1660s) have a parallel stem which spreads at the very top to form the Trefid end. As the pattern develops towards 1700 so the start of this spread moves further down the stem (Figure 71).

A more subtle change was that of bowl shape which gradually became more elongated over the same period (Figure 71).

The introduction of a rat tail on the back of the bowls of spoons of this pattern led to an alteration in the positioning of the hallmarks. Taking London as our example, early English and Puritan spoons had been marked with the leopard's head in the bowl of the spoon and the remaining marks on the back of the stem. Any attempt to strike the leopard's head, in its earlier position, on a Trefid spoon would have resulted in a damaged rat tail. It was, therefore, found necessary for this mark to be moved to join the others on the back of the stem. The marking of provincial examples was similarly modified although some examples, particularly West Country, had no rat tails.

Figure 71. *Trefid table spoons. Notice the development of both stem and bowl shape from the early example on the left to the latest on the right. Note also the positioning of the marks and the variations of the rat tail. Private collection.*

There are several variants of rat tail. The most usual are the plain ribbed rat tail and the beaded rat tail. A more rare type is the scroll decorated ribbed rat tail (Figure 72). A rare plain rat tail may also be found on late examples.

Apart from the important new positioning of the leopard's head mark, discussed above, there was a very useful development in the spacing of the marks struck on the back of the stem (see pp. 38-40).

From c.1660 on there was a gradual movement down the stem of the position of the date letter. At the same time the other marks became more spaced out. By about 1680 all the marks were positioned fairly evenly along the lower two-thirds of the stem. After this date a gradual move down the stem of the marks took place so that by 1700 the marks were grouped in the lower half of the stem (Figure 71).

The ends of Trefid spoons turn up when viewed from the front. The reason for this is that these spoons were placed on the table in the French manner with the back uppermost. It is for the same reason that the engravings of armorials, crests and initials are to be found, if original, on the back of the stem (Figures 71-74).

There are several interesting variants of Trefids in addition to those mentioned above.

Figure 72. *Trefid spoon with scroll decorated ribbed rat tail. London, 1682, Israel Pinkney (Kent). Courtesy Phillips.*

Figure 74. *Trefid spoon (lace back) with pips in the Trefid end. London, 1679, maker's mark NB. Courtesy Phillips.*

Figure 75. *Two from a set of six silver-gilt Trefid teaspoons. London, c.1690, five with maker's mark PH, one with maker's mark DS crowned. The bust engraved in the oval cartouche is usual on these delightful spoons. Courtesy Brand Inglis.*

Figure 73. *A late seventeenth century provincial lace back Trefid, West Country, Richard Sweet, the engravings on the back of the stem. Notice the positioning of the marks giving the visual impression of a set of hallmarks although the maker's mark only has been used struck three times. Private collection.*

Figure 76. *Silver-gilt, engraved foliate scroll Trefid spoon and fork, London, 1693, maker's mark TD in monogram. Private collection.*

An important early variety has small pips in the notches of the Trefid end (Figure 74). Later variations are engraved Trefids, lace back Trefids and flame back Trefids. Engraved examples are found mostly around the 1690s, lace backs and flame backs will be found earlier.

Engraved Trefids mostly employ foliate scroll motifs; otherwise cherubs and masks are sometimes found. A good many engraved examples are gilded (Figures 75 and 76). Sets of engraved and gilded teaspoons are found, often in small shagreen cases (Figure 75).

Lace back Trefids have their decoration produced by the bowl being hammered into a die in which the decoration has been cut (Figure 77). The more rare flame back is stamped on each side of the rat tail using the same technique as the lace backs (Figure 78).

Having examined the pattern in general, and Trefid spoons in particular, what of Trefid forks? These are very rare, the fork only just coming into general use in England at the end of the seventeenth century. When found, Trefid forks usually have three prongs (Figure 76), although occasionally, two and sometimes four-prong forks are found. Trefid forks do not have rat tails.

77

Figure 77. *Set of six lace back Trefids. London, 1686, maker's mark T crowned (attributed (Kent) to Thomas Issod). Courtesy Sotheby's.*

Figure 78. *Flame back Trefid. London, 1678, John King. A similar decoration is found on the top front of the stem. Courtesy Christie's.*

78

Figure 79. *Modern lace back Trefid; the spoon and fork are straight copies but the knife is an entirely modern version. Courtesy C.J. Vander.*

By the early 1700s the Trefid pattern was being rapidly superseded by the new Dog Nose pattern. The pattern was revived in the late nineteenth century and is still produced today (Figure 79).

Seventeenth century Trefid spoons are not normally collected as part of a flatware service but as individual items. There is no known complete service apart from those produced after the revival of the pattern. Building a service would be practically impossible and extremely expensive.

There are many combinations of the various types of rat tail, lace backs, engraving, with or without pips, etc. As a result Trefids are a fascinating group to collect as individual spoons. Once provincial variants are included the range is enormous.

Pitfalls

Condition, as always, is of paramount importance. Look particularly for repairs and splits in the bowl, especially next to the rat tail, and also along the stem. Look also for worn reshaped bowls indicated by thin whippy metal and unnatural hammer marks.

Engraved Trefids have to be examined closely to ensure that the decoration is original to the spoon. As regards engraving, also check armorials, crests and initials to see how contemporary these are.

Fakes are mostly produced by castings from original spoons (see pp. 67-9).

All late Trefid spoons (after 1700), especially if London made, should be regarded with great suspicion. This is because Dog Nose spoons and forks, until recently considerably cheaper than Trefids, have been converted to Trefids by cutting notches in their ends.

Dog Nose

During the reign of Queen Anne flatware was practically all of the Dog Nose pattern; this is easily recognised by the distinctive shape at the top of the stem. Sometimes, as a result of this shape, the pattern will be referred to as wavy end or shield end.

When studying the development of flatware this pattern provides an interesting transition between the Trefid and the Hanoverian. In essence, Dog Nose is the Trefid pattern without the notches cut into the end. Most was made between 1700 and 1715, though a few examples may be found from the late 1690s with some after 1715. The pattern was revived in the late nineteenth century and is still made today.

Plain or Basic

Early examples will have a stem of oblong cross section, following the style of the Trefid pattern. Late examples will normally have a stem of oval cross section. As with the Trefid there will be a rat tail on the back of the bowl which, with early examples, will be ribbed or, most usually, beaded, and with late examples will be plain (Figure 80 and back dust jacket).

Figure 80. *Queen Anne Dog Nose table spoons. Notice the flat stems on the early examples (1704) with beaded rat tails, and the narrow stems on the later (1709/10) plain rat tail examples. Courtesy Phillips.*

Dog Nose

The forks of this pattern normally have three prongs or tines (Figure 81) although four are known (Figure 82).

The knives associated with the Dog Nose are cannon handled (Figure 83) and pistol handled (Figure 84).

Crests, armorials and initials should be engraved on the back of the stem since during this period flatware was laid in the French manner, i.e. with spoon bowl facing down (Figure 85).

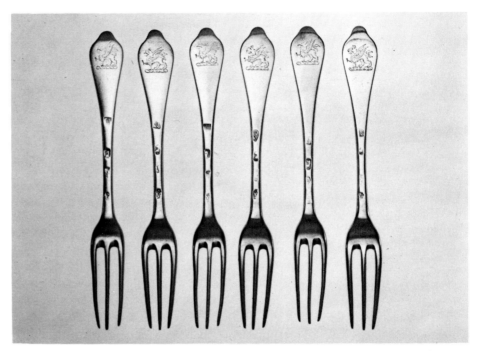

Figure 81. Six from a set of twelve Queen Anne Dog Nose table forks by Isaac Davenport, 1705 and 1707. These show the conventional three prongs and beginning of the narrowing down of the stem that one can expect to find about this date. Courtesy Christie's.

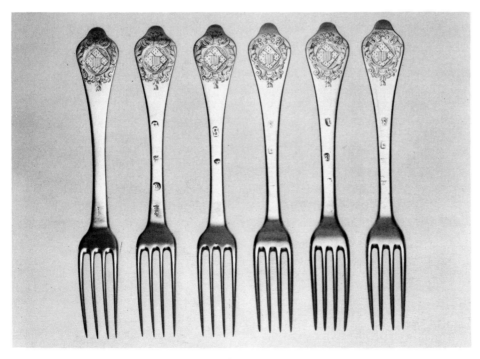

Figure 82. Six early (1695/97) and unusual four-pronged Dog Nose forks by Pierre Harache. Notice the early broad stems. Courtesy Christie's.

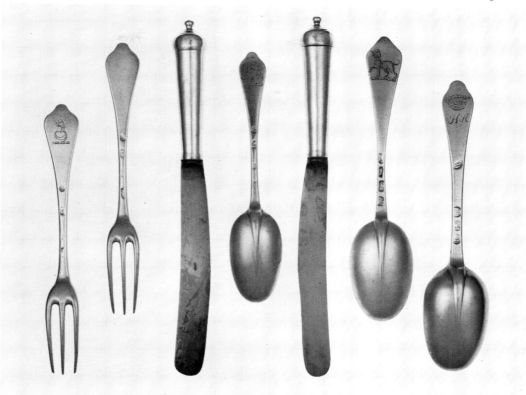

Figure 83.
*Examples of early
eighteenth century Dog
Nose pattern with
cannon handle knives.
Notice the crests
engraved on the backs
and the plain rat tails
on the spoons.
Courtesy Sotheby's.*

Figure 84. *Modern
examples of the Dog
Nose pattern with a
pistol handle knife.
Courtesy C.J.
Vander.*

Figure 85. *An
example of the Dog
Nose pattern produced
in Scotland. Two
from a set of twelve.
Glasgow, 1705, John
Luke Jnr. Courtesy
Sotheby's.*

This is the earliest pattern of which complete services exist though they are extremely rare, the majority of existing services being a mixture of dates and makers. However, with a great deal of patience, it would be possible to build an early eighteenth century service of this pattern.

Pitfalls

The greatest danger is that of cast fakes from existing genuine examples. This applies particularly to the forks which are the most difficult to find, especially the dessert size (see pp. 67 and 69).

Always be very suspicious of any gilded example; gilding has often been carried out in order to hide solder lines where they should not be.

Any example which falls outside the usual datelines, late 1690s to c.1720 and the second half of the nineteenth century to date, should be viewed with added caution.

Engraved Dog Nose

Early flat stem Dog Nose flatware is found with overall foliate engraving. Most examples are teaspoons and sweetmeat spoons and forks which can be found in small shagreen cases. The majority are gilded (Figure 86). Larger size spoons and forks are known but are rare. Building a service would not be possible.

Pitfalls

Look out for modern engraving, gilding and cast fakes.

Figure 86. *Set of six late seventeenth century silver-gilt engraved Dog Nose sweetmeat knives, forks and spoons. Maker's mark only PR, a coronet above. Courtesy Christie's.*

Beaded Dog Nose

An odd and rare Victorian variant of Dog Nose with a beaded edge and four-prong forks. Building a service would not be possible.

Pitfalls

As with all bead, make certain that the beading is in good condition.

Figure 87. *Beaded Dog Nose by Aldwinckle & Slater, London, 1886. Notice that the knife is pointed bead. Courtesy Sotheby's.*

Hanoverian

With and Without Rat Tail	Thread and Drop
Scottish Fiddle	Thread Shell and Drop (Lamerie)
Feather Edge and Shell	Thread Shell and Quilt (Quilted)
'Feather Edge Neptune Top'	Elizabethan
Military Thread	Venetian/Italian

The Hanoverian pattern can be said to be the most important flatware pattern of the eighteenth century. It first appeared in about 1710 and was produced up to the 1770s. Subsequently it was revived in the late nineteenth century and is still made today. The pattern evolved from the Dog Nose pattern, the top being rounded off.

Hanoverian With and Without Rat Tail

Although covering some sixty years the pattern may be divided into two principal groups: Hanoverian with rat tail, which may be dated to between 1710 and 1730 (this is often referred to as Rat Tail) (Figure 88), and Hanoverian without rat tail which dates from between about 1730 and 1770 (Figure 89).

Hanoverian without rat tail can be divided into three groups. These are single drop, double drop, and fancy or picture back. Single and double drop refer to the small heel which is the last vestige of the rat tail, and is either single (Figure 90) or double (Figure 91). With some late examples of double drop the second drop is often quite long (extended double drop) and generally rather weak. An extended single drop may also be found.

For fancy and picture backs see pp. 212-214.

There are other developments during the long period this pattern appeared. The most important of these is the rib on the front of the stem (Figures 92 and 93). With early examples this is very pronounced; the later the piece the less pronounced and the shorter, until, by the 1760s, it is reduced to a pip at the top of the stem.

The bowl also changes from an oval with early examples, to an egg shape with late ones.

Engraved crests, initials, etc., should be on the back of the stem.

Decorated examples will be found (Figure 94). Unless these are of a recognised pattern such as Lamerie (p. 91) or Elizabethan (pp. 92-3) it would be impossible to build a service.

Forks are three prong, with only rare exceptions. They also present the greatest danger, since they are probably the most extensively faked pieces of English silver (see p. 69).

The knives (pistol handle) to go with this pattern exist but are very rare.

Mixed services can be found.

Building a service is possible but very difficult.

See also Figures 95-97.

Pitfalls

Forgeries, particularly of forks (see p. 69).

Figure 88. *Hanoverian with rat tail or Rat Tail pattern table spoons and forks (part of a set of twelve of each). London, 1716. Courtesy Sotheby's.*

Figure 89. *Eighteenth century Hanoverian pattern without rat tails. The knives are octagonal pistol. Courtesy Sotheby's.*

Figure 90. *Hanoverian with single drop. Six table spoons, London, 1736, Isaac Callard. Courtesy Phillips.*

Figure 91. *Hanoverian with double drop. Four table spoons, London, 1734. Courtesy Phillips.*

Figure 92. *Very rare two-pronged dessert and table forks (part of a set of twelve of each), London, 1716/17, Thomas Burridge. Notice the pronounced rib on the front of the stem which is found with early examples of Hanoverian. Courtesy Sotheby's.*

93

Figure 93. *A Scottish example of Hanoverian without rat tail showing the rib on the front of the stem. Teaspoon mid-eighteenth century, maker's mark only AT. It is usual with small Scottish spoons of this period to find the maker's mark struck once only with no other marks. Courtesy M. McAleer.*

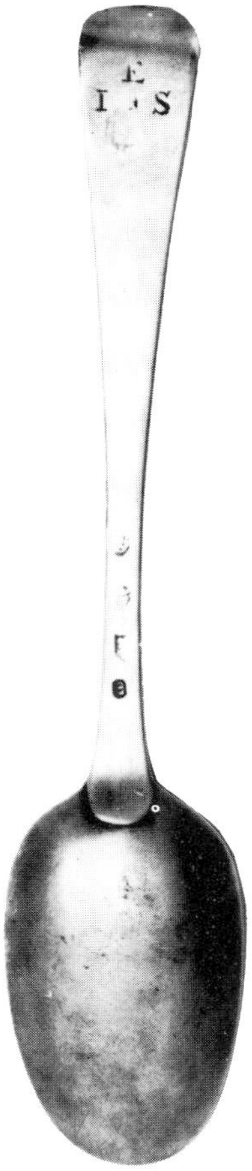

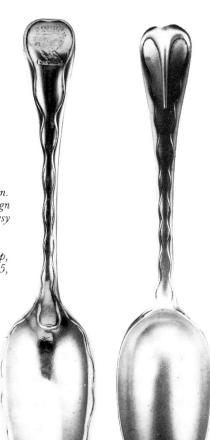

95

Figure 94. *Decorated Hanoverian table spoon. Unmarked, c.1730/40. This is the sort of design one would expect from Paul de Lamerie. Courtesy Henry Willis.*

Figure 95. *Irish Hanoverian single drop, without rat tail. Table spoon, Dublin, 1735, Isaac D'Olier. Courtesy M. McAleer.*

94

Figure 96. *A modern version of Hanoverian rat tail. Notice that four-prong (Old English type) forks have been used. Courtesy Phillips.*

Scottish Fiddle

A scarce variant of plain Hanoverian (with shaped handle) found mostly in Scandinavia but peculiar in the British Isles to Scotland. It dates from the mid-eighteenth century (Figure 98). Apart from teaspoons and mash spoons (see p. 207) very little will be found. Most examples are maker's mark only.

For Fiddle pattern made in Scotland see p. 59.

Hanoverian Feather Edge and Shell

A rare variant which appears in the 1760s. The illustrated example (Figure 99) has an almost straight stem. This is not surprising during the period of transition from Hanoverian to Old English.

Odd pieces may be found, but building a service would probably be impossible.

Hanoverian 'Feather Edge Neptune Top' (pattern of unknown name)

A pattern inspired by mid-eighteenth century decorated Hanoverian (Figure 100). It bears the PODR number 200,344 registered in 1892.

Figure 97. *Modern examples of the Hanoverian pattern. Courtesy C.J. Vander.*

Figure 98. *Scottish Fiddle pattern. Two teaspoons, left maker's mark only JW; right maker's mark only indistinct. Courtesy M. McAleer.*

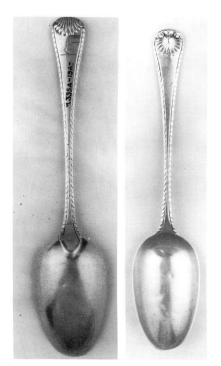

Figure 99. *Hanoverian Feather Edge and Shell. Table spoon, c.1760, marks indistinct. Courtesy Victoria and Albert Museum.*

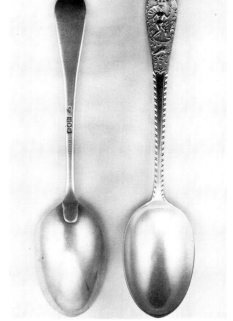

Figure 100. *Hanoverian 'Feather Edge Neptune Top'. Table spoons, London, 1905, Goldsmiths' and Silversmiths' Company. Courtesy Bourdon-Smith.*

99

100

Hanoverian Military Thread

A rare nineteenth century pattern.

Finding any pieces would be difficult and building a service probably impossible. See figure 101.

Pitfalls

Confusion with ordinary Thread; as with all 'military' patterns the thread edge ends in scrolls at the base of the stem.

Hanoverian Thread and Drop

A very rare pattern produced in about 1760 and copied by the Victorians.

Services from the eighteenth century, should they exist, would be extremely rare and to build a service would be impossible.

Turn of the nineteenth/twentieth century examples, both services and odd pieces, can be found.

See Figure 102.

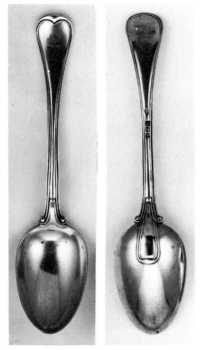

Figure 101. *Hanoverian Military Thread. Dessert spoon, London, 1906, HA&S. Courtesy Bruford and Heming.*

Figure 102. *Hanoverian Thread and Drop. Examples from a service, London, 1907, Francis Higgins. Courtesy Sotheby's.*

Figure 103. *Thread Shell and Drop (Lamerie). Part of a silver-gilt service engraved with a royal crest. London 1770/1844. Notice the use of three prongs for the fork. Courtesy Christie's.*

Figure 104. *Thread Shell and Drop (Lamerie). Part of a modern service with four-prong forks. London, 1919. Courtesy Sotheby's.*

Hanoverian Thread Shell and Drop (Lamerie)

A decorative version of Hanoverian pattern first produced in the mid-eighteenth century (examples are known by Isaac Callard); it has been produced intermittently to the present day. Known today as Lamerie, modern examples are machine made and hand finished.

Finding or building an old service would be extremely difficult.

Modern services and pieces can be found, and building a modern service would be possible although not easy.

See Figures 103 and 104.

Figure 105. *Hanoverian Thread Shell and Quilt (Quilted). Dessert spoon, London, 1895, TS, WS, MM. Table fork, London, 1841, by Geo. W. Adams. It is interesting to notice that the dessert spoon uses the union shell heel most often found during the Regency. Courtesy Victoria and Albert Museum.*

Hanoverian Thread Shell and Quilt (Quilted)

A rare nineteenth century pattern based on eighteenth century decorated Hanoverian which appears in the Chawner & Co. Pattern Book.

Services are known. Odd pieces may be found, but building a service would be very difficult.

See Figure 105 and p. 220.

Elizabethan (see also King's Shape 'Elizabethan' (p. 134) and Ornamental Elizabethan (p. 147))

A nineteenth century pattern which has no connection with the types of spoon produced in the reign of Queen Elizabeth I. The name results from the Renaissance form of decoration which appears on the stem — decorated Hanoverian would perhaps be a more apt name.

Chawner & Co. give this pattern as Elizabethan in their Pattern Book (see p. 217).

This pattern was first produced in about 1850 and is still made today.

Complete nineteenth century services exist but are scarce; however, it would be possible, although difficult, to construct a service.

See Figures 106 and 107 and front dust jacket.

Pitfalls

Could be confused with Venetian (p. 94) or King's Shape 'Elizabethan' (p. 134).

Figure 106. *Elizabethan. Part of an extensive silver-gilt dessert service by J. Garrard 1876/86/89. Courtesy Sotheby's.*

Figure 107. *Modern examples of the nineteenth century Elizabethan pattern. Courtesy C.J. Vander.*

Venetian/Italian

A mid-nineteenth century pattern the design for which was registered 18th February, 1868. Most nineteenth century pieces are by Martin Hall & Co. (Figure 108).

The distinction between Venetian and Italian is subtle. The basic design is the same but is more compact with Venetian. For example, look at the plain line surrounding the circular cartouche at the top of the stem. With Venetian the small scrolls at the end of the baroque decoration intrude into this plain line; with Italian there is a very slight gap between the scrolls and the circle.

Services, although scarce, can be found and building a service would be possible but not easy.

Figure 108. *Venetian pattern examples from a silver-gilt dessert service, London, 1873, Martin Hall & Co. (with some Sheffield 1872 pieces). Italian has the same design but with slightly greater spacing in the decoration. Courtesy Christie's.*

Old English

Plain or Basic
Pointed (Celtic Pointed)
With Shoulders
Admiralty (Crown and Anchor)
Bead
Bright-cut (including different Irish Pointed)
Bright-cut Edge
Feather Edge
Feather Edge with Shoulders
Feather Edge with Cartouche (Carrington Shield)
Shell
Thread
Laurel
Thread and Shell
Military Thread and Shell (Military Shell)
Coffin End

Old English ranks as one of the major flatware patterns and is, therefore, one of the most frequently encountered. It was first produced in about 1760 but may be found from earlier dates, particularly with serving pieces.

Old English Plain or Basic

The two important differences between this and the Hanoverian are, first, that the ends of the spoons turn down instead of up. Spoons from the introduction of this pattern were placed on the table open bowl uppermost. As a result crests and initials appear on the front of the spoon stems. Secondly, the forks become four-prong instead of three. They do, however, normally continue to turn up in the same way as the earlier three-prong examples. With forks the crests and initials continue to be engraved on the back of the stem. Occasionally turned down forks will be found (particularly by the Batemans); these are best avoided as they are very uncomfortable to use.

This pattern, which is still produced today, has many variants.

There are two variants of the basic pattern, those with rounded stems (normally c.1760-1800), and those with a more flattened stem (normally very early examples together with examples after 1800). The Chawner & Co. Pattern Book lists these as plain (round stem) and French (flat stem).

Another division that can be made with basic Old English pattern is with the positioning of the marks. In about 1784, when the duty mark first appeared, the hallmarks were moved from the bottom (Figure 109) to the top (Figure 19g) of the

Figure 109. *Old English bottom-marked dessert spoon with flat stem and extended single drop. London, 1771 (marks partially covered by sticky tape!). Courtesy Bruford and Heming.*

Figure 110. *Old English top marked with rounded stem and short single drop (for detail of back see Figures 29 and 30). Part of a service, London, 1786/96 by George Smith and William Fearn, with modern knives. Private Collection.*

stem. This saved a great deal of work for the spoon makers who had, with bottom marked examples, to restore the shape of the stem after marking. As a result it is necessary to distinguish between bottom marked Old English and top marked Old English. If you are building a service it is best to stick to one or the other.

As with Hanoverian, single and double drop heels will be found both short and extended.

The basic, plain, Old English is without doubt one of the best patterns to choose if building a service. Straight and mixed services may both be found.

See also Figure 111.

Figure 111. *Irish Old English pattern table fork. Dublin, 1801, James Keating. Courtesy M. McAleer.*

Pitfalls

The most important pitfall with this pattern is the conversion of Fiddle pattern by the removal of the shoulders and filing down of the end of the stem. Look for file marks at the bottom and top of the stem, also the proportions of the top. How well is it rounded? Does the pip at the back look as though its sides have been cut off? Another point to bear in mind is that the top of the stem of Old English is normally thicker than Fiddle. Examples of this type of conversion will date from after 1800 and will naturally be of the oblong cross section.

Any Old English dated before 1760 must be examined with great care. When the pattern became popular services of the earlier Hanoverian were modernised by hammering the end on a stake to convert the turned up end into a turned down end.

In 1769 Isaac Callard's account with Parker & Wakelin includes '12 Table Spoons Reversed' (Garrard Mss., Victoria and Albert Museum). When this has been done the pip at the top of the stem generally looks quite weak. There are often the remains of the original crest or initials showing on the back of the stem.

Pointed Old English (Celtic Pointed)

The majority of Old English pattern flatware made in Ireland is the pointed end variant (Figure 112; also Figures 120-123, 125 and 126), as is a good amount of Scottish. Recently the name Celtic Pointed has been given to this pattern.

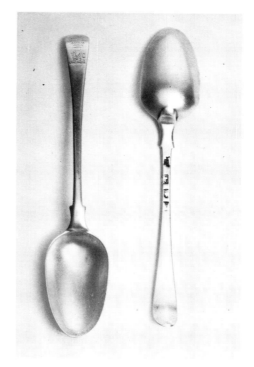

Figure 112. *Irish Pointed Old English. Left, set of four teaspoons, Cork, c.1800, Joseph Gibson. Right, pair of teaspoons, Cork, c.1790, James Warner. Courtesy Phillips.*

Figure 113. *Old English with Shoulders, bottom marked. Pair dessert spoons, London, 1763, Thomas and William Chawner. Courtesy Phillips.*

It was used for most of the fine Irish bright-cut patterns such as Star bright-cut and Plumes bright-cut.

Building services is possible with the plain form and with the more common Star bright-cut (see Figures 124 and 125), but becomes more difficult with the rarer bright-cuts such as Bow (see Figure 121), Flower Head (see Figure 122) or Plumes (see Figure 123).

Pitfalls

With bright-cut look out for modern engraving.

Old English with Shoulders

This is the first variant of the Old English patterns and mostly dates from around 1760/70. The marks in this variant will be at the bottom of the stem (Figure 113).

In 1770 Isaac Callard supplied Parker & Wakelin with twelve teaspoons 'with shoulders' (Garrard Mss., Victoria and Albert Museum).

Most of the pieces to be found will be spoons. Complete services are scarce and building a service would, therefore, be very difficult.

The number of pieces in this interesting style are diminishing, since people remove the shoulders to create the easier-to-match Old English without shoulders.

Figure 114. *Mid-nineteenth century Admiralty pattern flatware. Courtesy M. McAleer.*

Figure 115. *Detail showing the London marks for 1855, the maker Geo. W. Adams of Chawner & Co. Notice the broad arrow struck with the marks indicating Navy issue. Courtesy M. McAleer.*

Admiralty (Royal Navy, Old English with Crowned Fouled Anchor, Crown and Anchor)

This is a rare pattern. It is Old English, die stamped at the top of the stem with a crowned fouled anchor (Figure 114) and was first made for issue to the Navy for the use of officers in the first half of the nineteenth century, the earliest known examples being teaspoons of 1838.

Its issue to officers appears to have ceased at about the time of the First World War when it is believed serving officers were given the opportunity of purchasing sets, but services continue to be used in the Royal Navy messes, in particular on the Royal Yacht *Britannia,* H.M.S. *Victory,* and at the Royal Naval College, Dartmouth.

In addition to the usual maker's mark and hallmarks, Navy issue pieces will be stamped with the broad arrow (Figure 115).

Up to the mid-nineteenth century surviving pieces are by G.W. Adams of Chawner & Co. In the later 1850s and 1860s pieces by J.S. Hunt of Hunt & Roskell are found (these will have been made by Chawner & Co.), and in the 1870s by Francis Higgins and subsequently by Walker & Hall.

During the twentieth century this pattern has been produced in electro-plate.

Mixed services exist but are rare, so building a service would be difficult.

Old English Bead

The true period of this style was during the 1780s, although it is also found later, a good many pieces being produced in the nineteenth century.

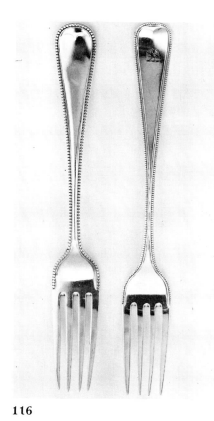

Figure 116. *Old English Bead table forks. Left, large bead, nineteenth century. Right, fine bead, eighteenth century. Courtesy Bruford and Heming.*

Figure 117. *Modern examples of Old English Bead pattern. The knife is pointed bead. Courtesy C.J. Vander.*

116   117

Two types of bead will be found: fine bead which dates from the eighteenth century and large bead which dates from the nineteenth (Figure 116).

A further distinction can be made between standard round-end bead and pointed bead which has a more pointed end to the stem (see the knife in Figure 117).

The pattern is still produced today (Figure 117).

Services exist but are scarce. It is possible, although difficult, to build a service.

Pitfalls

Finding pieces in good condition is a problem, the beaded edges being particularly prone to wear; always examine these very carefully.

Old English Bright-cut (see also Old English Bright-cut Edge, pp. 102-3)

This variant of Old English is mostly found from the 1790s and early 1800s, and is still produced today. It is distinguished from other Old English by the front of the stem being bright-cut engraved, and always on flat stem Old English. With bright-cut engraving facets, rather than lines, were cut into the surface of the silver. It is, in a sense, a form of carving a surface. Since the facets are cut at different angles, light is reflected at various angles and the decoration (when clean) appears to be sparkling, hence the name bright-cut.

This decorative technique is first found in about 1770 and resulted from the improvements in the cutting edges which could be achieved with better quality steel. Any example of silver with bright-cutting of mid-eighteenth century date or earlier must have been later engraved.

Eighteenth century services exist but are rare. Building a service is very difficult for two reasons. First, bright-cut forks are very difficult to find. Secondly, the styles vary so much. In fact, should you be brave enough to attempt such a venture, you should accept that the bright-cut designs will vary.

See Figures 118-125.

In recent years examples of plain Old English pattern have been bright-cut; these are not as valuable as the genuine examples and can generally be detected by comparing the sharpness of engraving with the degree of wear on the spoon or fork. In the same way some genuine, but worn, examples have been sharpened up.

Pitfalls

Plain, eighteenth century Old English pattern with modern bright-cut engraving.

Figure 118. *Bright-cut Old English pattern. Set of six table spoons, London, 1783, Hester Bateman. Courtesy Phillips.*

Figure 119. *Bright-cut Old English pattern. 'Set' of six teaspoons, London, 1787, Hester Bateman. Notice that what appears, at first glance, to be a straight set has one odd spoon with a different bright-cut pattern. It is quite probable that this set was originally supplied in this way by mistake. Courtesy Phillips.*

Figure 120. *Bright-cut Irish Pointed Old English. Six table spoons, Cork, c.1785, Carden Terry. Courtesy Phillips.*

121   122

Figure 121. *Bright-cut Irish pointed Old English Bow. Teaspoon, Dublin, c.1790, John Daly. Courtesy M. McAleer.*

Figure 122. *Bright-cut Irish Old English Flower Head. Pair dessert spoons, Dublin, 1798, J. Scott. Courtesy M. McAleer.*

Figure 123. *Bright-cut Irish pointed Old English Plumes. Set of six table spoons, Dublin, 1803, maker's mark script JK. Courtesy Phillips.*

Figure 125. *Bright-cut Irish pointed Old English Star. Set of six teaspoons, Dublin, c.1790, John Keen. Courtesy Phillips.*

Figure 124. *Bright-cut Irish pointed Old English Star. Soup ladle, Dublin, late eighteenth century. Courtesy M. McAleer.*

Old English Bright-cut Edge (see also Old English Feather Edge below)

This Old English variant mostly dates from the 1790s and early 1800s and will always be on flat stem Old English. It has been produced intermittently ever since it first appeared and is still made today. It appears in the Chawner & Co. Pattern Book as Bright Engraved Edge (see p. 217).

This pattern is listed in late nineteenth/early twentieth century pattern books as Edinburgh or New Edinboro' [sic].

Services both straight and mixed exist but are quite scarce.

There is less of a problem of matching when building a service with this than with Old English Bright-cut since there is less variation in the number of styles.

See Figures 126 and 127.

Pitfalls

See Old English Bright-cut pitfalls (p. 100).

Old English Feather Edge (see also Old English Feather Edge with Shoulders, p. 105)

Principally dating from the 1770s, this pattern has been produced intermittently to

Figure 126. *Bright-cut Edge Irish pointed Old English. Six from a set of twelve dessert spoons, Dublin, c.1785, John Pittar. Courtesy Phillips.*

Figure 128. *Modern examples of Old English Feather Edge. Courtesy C.J. Vander.*

Figure 127. *Modern examples of Old English Bright-cut Edge. Courtesy C.J. Vander.*

Figure 129. *Old English Feather Edge with Shoulders, ordinary type with the feather-edging on shoulders and stem cut in the same direction. Dessert spoon, London 1770. Courtesy Sotheby's.*

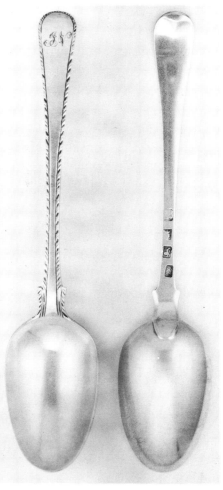

Figure 130. *Old English Feather Edge with Shoulders, alternate type with the feather-edging on shoulders cut in the opposite direction to that on the stem. Pair of table spoons, London, 1768, John Lampfert. Courtesy C.J. Vander.*

Figure 131. *Old English Feather Edge and Cartouche (Carrington Shield). Table forks without shoulders, London, 1894, Carrington. Courtesy Commercial Smelting Company.*

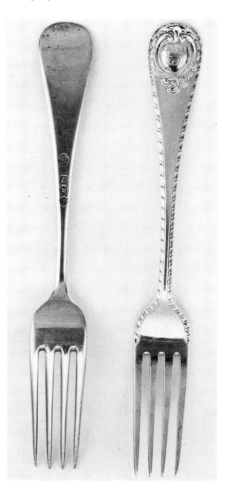

the present day. It is distinguished from other Old English variants by the feather-like edge engraving, of which there are two types: (1) Ordinary. The feather-edging all cut in the same direction up the handle (Figure 128). (2) Alternate. The upper part cut as in the ordinary form, the lower part of the stem cut in the opposite direction (see Figure 130).

In 1766 William and Thomas Chawner supplied Parker & Wakelin with 'Gadrooned spoons' (Garrard Mss., Victoria and Albert Museum). This may refer to what is known today as Feather Edge.

Supporting evidence is to be found in the Chawner & Co. Pattern Book where this pattern (ordinary form) is listed as Gadroon Edge (see p. 217).

Services exist but are scarce. Building one is possible but difficult.

Pitfalls

Beware of modern feather-edging on 1770s plain Old English. Look to see if the amount of wear on the decoration is the same as the wear on the spoon bowls and the tines of the forks; with later engraved examples one often sees sharp decoration on worn pieces. Beware, too, of examples which have been 'sharpened up', i.e. worn examples re-engraved.

Old English Feather Edge with Shoulders (see also Old English Feather Edge, p. 102)

This scarce pattern was produced only around the 1770s and is distinguished from Old English Feather Edge by the shoulders at the bottom of the stem.

There are two types: (1) Ordinary. The feather-edging on the shoulders and the handle cut in the same direction (Figure 129). (2) Alternate. The feather-edging on the shoulders cut in the opposite direction to that on the handle (Figure 130).

Services exist but are rare. Building a service is possible but would be difficult.

Pitfalls

Beware of examples which have been 'sharpened up', i.e. worn examples re-engraved. Beware, too, of Plain Old English with shoulders which has been engraved to match an existing service of this pattern (see Old English Feather Edge Pitfalls, p. 104).

Old English Feather Edge and Cartouche (Carrington Shield)

First produced around the 1770s (pieces are known by Thomas Northcote) this pattern is found in two forms, with and without shoulders (Figure 131). A variant of the form with shoulders is known with scrolls at the shoulders.

The pattern was revived in the late nineteenth century by Carrington — hence its alternative name — and is still available today.

Odd early pieces can be found but building an early service would probably not be possible.

It would be possible, but very difficult, to build a secondhand service. Better to buy a complete service.

Old English Shell

A rare variant of the Old English pattern distinguished by the shell at the top of the stem. It is found first in the 1770s but was mostly produced during the Victorian period and is still produced today.

Eighteenth century services are very rare, and it would be almost impossible to build one.

Nineteenth century services are scarce, and building one would be possible but difficult.

See Figure 132.

Old English Thread (see also Hanoverian Thread and Drop, p. 90)

This Old English variant dates principally from the late eighteenth century. In 1767 Isaac Callard supplied Wakelin with 'Threaded Table Spoons', and in 1772 Philip Rainaud supplied '12 Large threaded Coffee Spoons 11oz 17'. (Garrard Mss., Victoria and Albert Museum.)

An invoice of Clarke & Green (retailers) dated 27th July, 1787 includes '24 double threaded polished Silver table spoons Double threaded each side.'

Both double and single struck will be found, and normally the edge will have a double thread. The Chawner & Co. Pattern Book lists this as Straight Double Threaded. On rare occasions a single thread may be found.

Figure 132. *Modern examples of Old English Shell. Courtesy C.J. Vander.*

Figure 134. *Modern examples of Old English Thread and Shell. Courtesy C.J. Vander.*

Figure 133. *Modern examples of Old English Thread. Courtesy C.J. Vander.*

Figure 135. *Old English Coffin End teaspoon, London, 1808, Thomas Wallis. Courtesy Henry Willis.*

The pattern has been produced intermittently ever since it first appeared and is still made today.

Eighteenth and early nineteenth century services can be found but are scarce. It is possible, although difficult, to build a service. Of all the Old English variants this is probably the easiest to find.

See Figure 133.

Pitfalls

The author has seen attempts to engrave a thread edge on to Plain Old English. This has always been done badly and should be quite obvious to anyone collecting a service.

Laurel

The identification of eighteenth century Laurel pattern flatwares presents a problem.

In 1768 William Portal (see pp. 47-8) supplied Parker & Wakelin with 'Lawrel'd Knives'. The following year William and Thomas Chawner's account with Parker & Wakelin includes 'By Lawrelling 12 Dessert Spoons'. Wood & Filkins' account in 1771 includes '12 Laurelled Shell Teaspoons' (Garrard Mss., Victoria and Albert Museum).

A possible contender would be the Feather Edge pattern which was certainly in production at the time. The same accounts however refer to 'gadrooned' pieces, which would describe the Feather Edge pattern better than a laurelled pattern.

Occasionally Old English is found with an engraved edge which may be the Laurel pattern of the eighteenth century. This consists of a thread edge with what appear to be laurel leaves engraved at intervals.

Not illustrated.

Old English Thread and Shell

A rare variant of Old English first produced in about 1770. It has been produced intermittently since and is still made today.

Eighteenth century services are extremely rare, but a York-made service is known. Building an eighteenth century service would be extremely difficult.

See Figure 134.

Old English Military Thread and Shell (Military Shell)

A rare pattern illustrated in the Chawner & Co. Pattern Book (see Appendix, p. 218).

Any services or pieces are rare, and building a service would be extremely difficult.

Pitfalls

Confusion with Old English Thread and Shell.

Coffin End

A rare variant of the Old English pattern with squared off end and canted sides to the top giving the handle a coffin-like appearance. Examples date mostly from around 1800.

Building a service would be impossible.

See Figure 135.

Pitfalls

Plain Old English which has been filed later to a Coffin End.

Figure 136. *A French Fiddle pattern table spoon, Paris, 1738/44, Charles Girrard. Courtesy Phillips.*

Figure 137. *Fiddle pattern table spoon, London, 1739, Isaac Callard. This is the earliest known English example of this pattern. Notice that the end turns up in the French manner and that it has no shoulders. It was probably made to replace a lost piece from a French service. Courtesy Thomas Lumley Ltd.*

136   137

Fiddle

Plain or Basic	Fiddle and Shell
Without Shoulders (Oar pattern)	Thread
Husk	Military Thread
Military Husk	Thread and Drop
Husk Plain Stem	Thread and Shell

Plain or Basic (see also Fiddle without Shoulders, p. 111)

Deriving its name from its fiddle-shaped handle, the Fiddle pattern must rate as one of the major designs for flatware.

Perhaps the earliest example is to be found amongst the Esquiline Treasure of late Roman silver in the British Museum. Its production in England did not however stem directly from this source but from France where, in the mid-eighteenth century, it was the most popular pattern (Figure 136).

In 1769 William and Thomas Chawner supplied Parker & Wakelin with Fiddle Pattern flatware:

1769
22nd May 12 French Table 4 prong forks }
       "   "   Table spoons   } Fiddle Heads

(Garrard Mss., Workmen's Ledger No. 2, Victoria and Albert Museum).

With Fiddle pattern and all its derivatives there are two types which may be found. These are English style where the spoons turn down and the forks up, and French style where both spoons and forks turn up and the shoulders are usually much softer. The vast majority of pieces found are of English style, French being quite scarce.

Some examples can be found from the eighteenth century. A table spoon by Isaac Callard dated 1739 is the earliest known example from the British Isles and was probably made to replace a lost piece from a French service (Figure 137).

However, the vast majority of Fiddle pattern dates from after 1800 when, with the change to the heavier classicism of the Regency, the pattern rapidly replaced the lighter forms of the Old English.

After the middle years of the nineteenth century its popularity began to wane and in the early twentieth century it was produced only intermittently. Today it is the only major flatware pattern not in production, although several of its decorative variants such as Fiddle Thread and Shell are still produced.

It is interesting to note that most nineteenth century flatware patterns developed either directly or indirectly from the Fiddle.

The Flatware produced for Admiral Lord Nelson was of this pattern as was the Chawner family's personal service (Figure 17).

Many services both straight and mixed exist and it is probably the best of all patterns from which to build services.

See Figures 136-142.

Pitfalls

When building a service do not mix London, provincial, Scottish and Irish since the proportions of Fiddle vary quite considerably depending on where a piece was made (see Figure 140).

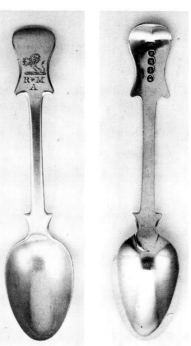

Figure 138. *A mixed group of plain English style nineteenth century Fiddle pattern. Courtesy Phillips.*

Figure 139. *An odd, quite possibly unique, variant of the Fiddle pattern. London, 1826, William Traies. Courtesy Henry Willis.*

Figure 140. *Set of four Fiddle pattern Scottish toddy ladles. Aberdeen, c.1800, James Erskine. In the centre, one of a pair of Fiddle pattern Scottish toddy ladles. Dundee, c.1815, maker's mark WL. Notice the quite different proportions of the Fiddle pattern between the central (English proportioned) ladle and the other (Scottish proportioned) four. See also p. 59. Courtesy Phillips.*

Figure 141. *Interesting Scottish examples of Fiddle pattern. Aberdeen, George Sangster, with Edinburgh hallmarks of 1850. The proportions are English. For an interesting comparison of English and Scottish proportions see Figure 140. Courtesy M. McAleer.*

Figure 142. *Irish provincial Fiddle pattern. Pair of table forks, Cork, c.1810, John Seymour. Notice the rib extending from the pip at the top of the stem. Courtesy M. McAleer.*

Fiddle without Shoulders (Oar pattern)

A fairly scarce variant of Fiddle pattern (Figure 143) sometimes called Oar pattern (particularly in Scotland). It dates mostly from about 1800/5 when Fiddle first became really popular in England. Scottish examples will be found well into the nineteenth century — Figures 144 and 145.

Services exist but are rare.

It is possible to build up a service but it would be far more difficult than ordinary Fiddle.

Pitfalls

Beware of ordinary Fiddle that has had its shoulders removed. These alterations will mostly be found in made-up services.

Figure 145. *Fiddle without Shoulders (Oar pattern). Gravy spoon, Scottish proportions, Perth, c.1820, R. Keay. Courtesy Phillips.*

Figure 143. *Fiddle without Shoulders (Oar pattern). Set of four teaspoons, Newcastle, 1827, Thomas Wheatley. Courtesy M. McAleer.*

Figure 144. *Fiddle without Shoulders (Oar pattern). Dessert spoons, English proportions, Glasgow, 1853, maker's mark PA. Courtesy M. McAleer.*

Figure 146. *Left, Fiddle Husk with thread heel. Dessert fork, London, 1837, Mary Chawner. Right, Fiddle Husk with husk heel. Table spoon, London, 1826, Charles Eley. Courtesy Bruford and Heming.*

Figure 147. *Part of a Fiddle Husk service, the majority by William Traies, London, 1842. Courtesy Sotheby's.*

Fiddle Husk (Husk Shell in the Chawner & Co. Pattern Book)

A scarce early nineteenth century variant of the Fiddle pattern often confused with Fiddle Thread and Shell (p. 118). The distinguishing feature is the shell which, in this case, is the more elaborate 'husk' type. (Compare Figures 147 and 151.)

This pattern is still made today in a limited range of pieces.

There are two variants of this pattern, husk heel and thread heel (see Figure 146), husk being the standard type.

Services exist but are rare. Building a service would be possible but difficult.

Pitfalls

Confusion with Fiddle Thread and Shell and with Military Fiddle Husk.

Military Fiddle Husk

A rare variant of Fiddle Husk distinguished from the standard pattern by the small scrolls at the base of the stem instead of the usual shoulders (Figure 148).

Services may exist; building a service would be almost impossible.

Pitfalls

Confusion with both ordinary Fiddle Husk and with Fiddle Thread and Shell.

Fiddle Husk Plain Stem

A very rare Fiddle variant often confused with the Fiddle and Shell pattern from which it is distinguished by its husk-type shell. It is found both double and single struck (Figure 149).

Services may exist; building a service would be almost impossible.

Pitfalls

Confusion with Fiddle and Shell pattern.

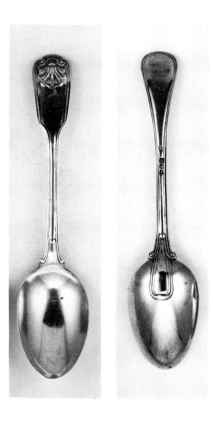

Figure 148. *Military Fiddle Husk. Dessert spoon, London, 1847, Geo. W. Adams of Chawner & Co. Courtesy Bruford and Heming.*

Figure 149. *Left, single struck Fiddle Husk plain stem. Table spoon, London, 1830, William Traies. Right, double struck Fiddle Husk plain stem. Dessert spoon, London, 1835, Charles Boyton. Courtesy Commercial Smelting Co.*

Figure 150. *Single struck Fiddle and Shell. Table spoons from an extensive service. London, 1843. Courtesy Bourdon-Smith.*

Figure 151. *Double struck Fiddle and Shell with Union shell heel. Table forks, London, 1818, Wms. Eley & Fearn. Courtesy C.J. Vander.*

Fiddle and Shell

This is a scarce variant of Fiddle pattern dating from the early nineteenth century and made mostly in Scotland and Newcastle, although London examples will be found.

The majority of items are single struck (Figure 150), although rare double struck examples can be found (Figure 151).

Services do exist but are quite scarce. It would be possible and not too difficult to build a service.

See also Figure 152.

Pitfalls

If building a service try not to mix Scottish examples with English as the proportions are usually rather different; it is best to stick to one or the other. Confusion with plain Fiddle Husk could be a problem.

Fiddle Thread (see also Military Thread, p. 117)

This is one of the most popular basic variants of Fiddle pattern dating from about 1805 and still produced today. Occasionally eighteenth century examples may be found.

There are a number of variants. Both French and English type (see p. 108) will be found as will double and single struck (Figure 153). Paul Storr in particular produced a rather fine French style Fiddle Thread.

Chawner & Co. list this pattern as Double Threaded Fiddle in their Pattern Book (p. 218).

Many services exist both mixed and straight; it is one of the best patterns for building a service.

See Figures 153-158.

Pitfalls

Mixing French and English type can be a problem.

Look for wear on the thread edges, particularly at the top where the removal of a crest may have resulted in damage.

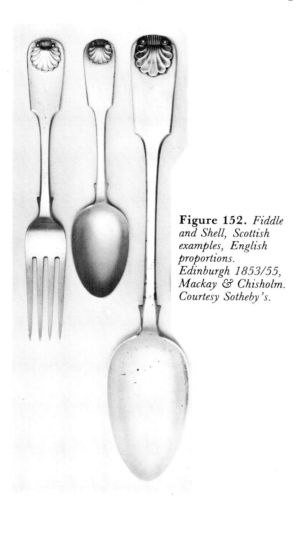

Figure 152. *Fiddle and Shell, Scottish examples, English proportions. Edinburgh 1853/55, Mackay & Chisholm. Courtesy Sotheby's.*

Figure 153. *Unusually proportioned eighteenth century single struck Fiddle Thread with French (soft) shoulders. Pair of teaspoons, London, 1790, Peter and Jonathan Bateman. Courtesy Henry Willis.*

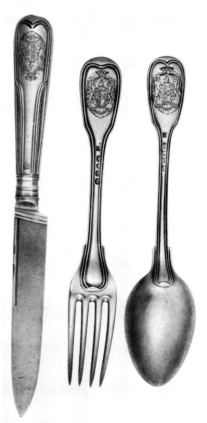

Figure 154. *The spoon an unusual variant of Fiddle Thread made to match an earlier Austrian service of which the fork is an example. Notice that there are no shoulders and that a single thread has been used. Silver-gilt. Engraved with the Royal crest the spoon is by Wms. Eley & Fearn, London, 1801. Courtesy Sotheby's.*

Figure 155. *French style Fiddle Thread. Notice that the spoon turns up, also the soft (French) shoulders and the attempt with the knife to produce a true Fiddle Thread pattern. Silver-gilt. Made by Wms. Eley & Fearn in 1822 to match an earlier French service. Courtesy Sotheby's.*

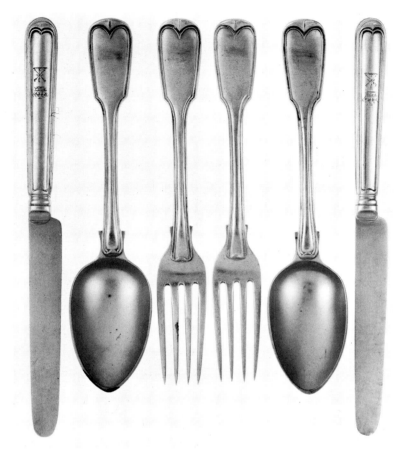

Figure 156. *French style Fiddle Thread; notice the English (hard) shoulders. London, 1840/41, Geo. W. Adams of Chawner & Co. Courtesy Sotheby's.*

Figure 157. *A very unusual variant of English style Fiddle Thread with very hard angles, no shoulders and a very fine thread. Avoid such an oddity if you are building a service. Mixed dates and makers, 1806/1872. Courtesy Sotheby's.*

Figure 158. *Modern examples of the Fiddle Thread pattern. Courtesy C.J. Vander.*

Figure 159. *Military Thread gravy spoon. London, mid-nineteenth century. Courtesy Phillips.*

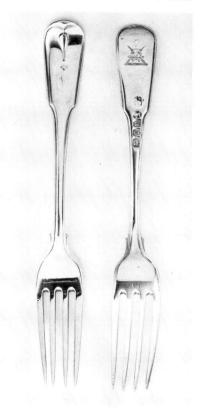

Figure 160. *Fiddle Thread and Drop. Notice that these are single thread and have French (soft) shoulders. Pair dessert forks, London, 1795, George Smith & Wm. Fearn. Courtesy C.J. Vander.*

Military Fiddle Thread (see also Fiddle Thread)

Military Thread is a scarce variant of the Fiddle Thread pattern — the difference between Fiddle Thread and Military Thread, as with all 'military' variants, being scrolls instead of shoulders (Figure 159).

Services exist, but building a service would be difficult.

Fiddle Thread and Drop

A rare variety of Fiddle Thread which dates from the late eighteenth and the early nineteenth century.

Services and individual pieces are rarely seen; building a service would be almost impossible.

See figure 160.

Pitfalls

As for Fiddle Thread.

Figure 161. *Left, Fiddle Thread and Shell with rare thread heel. Dessert spoon, London, 1821, Wms. Eley & Fearn. Centre, standard diamond heel. Notice that this has a convex shell at the top of the stem unlike the other two which are both concave. Dessert spoon, London, 1838. Right, scarce Union shell. Table spoon, London, 1807, Mary Sumner. Courtesy Bruford and Heming.*

Figure 162. *Fiddle Thread and Shell pattern; the standard form with diamond heel. London, 1850/51, Geo. W. Adams of Chawner & Co. Courtesy Sotheby's.*

Fiddle Thread and Shell

Dating from about 1810 and still produced today this is one of the most popular Fiddle pattern variants.

There are three basic variants: diamond heel, the most common; Union shell, which is quite scarce, and the rare thread heel (Figures 161 and 162).

Chawner & Co. list this pattern as Shell in their Pattern Book.

Many services exist both straight and mixed.

This is a good pattern to choose when building a service.

Pitfalls

Confusion with Fiddle Husk or Military Fiddle Husk, otherwise as for Fiddle Thread pitfalls.

King's Shape

Hourglass
King's
King's Honeysuckle
Queen's or Rosette
Scroll Rosette
Decorative King's Variants: Double Shell and Laurel
                      With Husk Shells
                      Dolphin
                      Princess No. 2
                      Pattern of unknown name
King's Shape Patterns: Classic Decoration: Bacchanalian
                                     Boar Hunt and Mask
                                     Fox Hunt
                                     Stag Hunt
                     Symbolic Decoration: Old England
                                     'Star and Cornucopia'
                       Botanic Decoration: 'Laurel'
                                     Rose
                                     Bright Vine
                                     'Trailing Vine'
                                     Chased Vine
                                     Pierced Vine
                       Formal Decoration: Coburg
                                     King's Shape 'Elizabethan'
                                     Plantagenet
                       Rococo Decoration: Cambridge
                                     King's Shape 'Rococo'
                                     'Scottish King's Shape' Rococo End
                                     Pattern of unknown name
King's Shape Double Threaded
King's Husk
King's Husk Variants: Plain Edge
                      Reverse
King's Husk Without Husk
Patterns developing from King's Husk Without Husk: Adelaide
                                                 Princess No. 1
                                                 Devonshire
                                                 Albert and Classic
                                                 Victoria
See also Louis XIV (p. 160) and XV (p. 146 and Figure 225)
            Rich Bead (Figure 232)
            Pattern of unknown name (Figure 239)

The three principal patterns in this group (which originate from French eighteenth century designs) are Hourglass, King's, and Queen's or Rosette. Since there is a good deal of confusion between all three a comparison of the standard forms will be useful at this point.

All three of the principal patterns have a stem, the top half of which has a shaped outline, the top decorated with a shell, while the base has shoulders. A decorative device is also to be found about one third of the way down the stem.

Of the above features it is best to look at the shells and decorative devices to distinguish between the three patterns.

The Hourglass pattern derives its name from the hourglass-like device about one third of the way down the stem. The shell on the front of the stem is concave, i.e. depressed into the surface as though looking at the inside of a scallop shell. The shell on the back is convex, i.e. raised from the surface as though looking at the outside of the shell.

King's pattern is distinguished from Hourglass by honeysuckle in place of the hourglass device. All other features are the same.

Queen's or Rosette pattern takes the elaboration of this design a stage further. The decoration is more pronounced than that of either Hourglass or King's. Both front and back shells are convex and a flower head is placed in the centre of the honeysuckle decoration.

These important distinguishing features are summarised as follows:

Pattern*	Hourglass	King's	Queen's or Rosette
Device	Hourglass	Honeysuckle	Flower head and honeysuckle
Front shell	Concave	Concave	Convex
Back shell	Convex	Convex	Convex

* Standard forms; some variants may differ.

Hourglass

A Regency pattern originating from French eighteenth century flatware. It has been produced steadily from the early nineteenth century to the present day. Occasionally eighteenth century English and Scottish examples may be found.

It is distinguished from King's and Queen's by the hourglass-like device about one third of the way down the item.

There are three variants to be found (see Figure 163):

(1) Standard with diamond heel (common).

(2) Union shell (scarce).

(3) Thread heel (rare).

Many services both straight and mixed, exist. The diamond heel Hourglass is one of the best patterns for building a service.

See also Figures 164 and 165.

Pitfalls

Confusion with King's pattern.

King's

This is one of the most popular of all flatware patterns, dating principally from the early nineteenth century, although occasionally, since it is based on French eighteenth century designs, earlier examples may be found. Large quantities of this pattern were produced throughout the nineteenth century, and are still being made today.

There are two basic types of this pattern when double struck:

(1) Diamond heel, which is the standard form.

(2) Union shell heel which is mostly found on earlier examples.

Single struck King's pattern also has two types: those with and those without

Figure 163. *Hourglass pattern. Left, diamond heel. Dessert fork, London, 1841, Wm. Eley; centre, Union shell heel. Dessert fork, London, 1843. Geo. W. Adams; right, thread heel. Dessert spoon, London, 1800, William Sumner. Courtesy Bruford and Heming.*

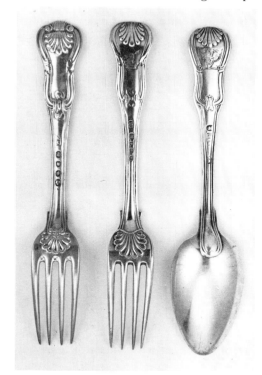

Figure 164. *Early nineteenth century Hourglass pattern service with modern knives. Private collection.*

Figure 165. *Modern C.J. Vander examples of the Hourglass pattern. Courtesy C.J. Vander.*

Figure 166. *Left, King's pattern with diamond heel; right, King's pattern with Union shell heel. Notice that the top shell is convex with the standard diamond heel and concave with the Union shell heel. Courtesy Bruford and Heming.*

Figure 167. *King's pattern. Part of a table service of standard form. Courtesy James Charles.*

Figure 168. *King's pattern with Union shell heel. Part of a silver-gilt dessert service, eighteen of each, London, 1815, Wms. Eley & Fearn. Courtesy Christie's.*

shoulders. The Chawner Pattern Book lists these as King's Front French Shoulder and King's Front Round Handle respectively.

Services both straight and mixed are quite easily found.

This is one of the easiest patterns for building a service.

See Figures 166-172 for examples.

Pitfalls

Confusion with both the Hourglass and the Queen's pattern is common (see p. 120).

It is best not to mix Scottish and English King's pattern since the Scottish is generally single struck and frequently has a simplified (round handle) version of the design.

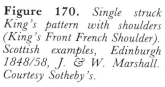

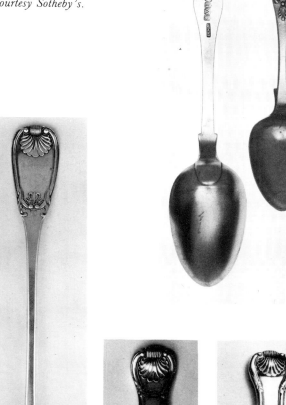

Figure 169. *Single struck King's pattern with shoulders. Part of a service, London, 1875, Francis Higgins. Courtesy Sotheby's.*

Figure 171. *A variant of King's pattern. Scottish single struck with shoulders. The term Bastard (see p. 72) has been used for many years for such a variant, thus: 'Scottish Bastard King's' would be a correct description of this spoon. Gravy spoon, Glasgow, 1823, Robert Gray & Son. Courtesy Bruford and Heming.*

Figure 172. *Irish King's pattern with Union Shell heel. Dublin, 1829, James Brady with Neill as retailer. Courtesy M. McAleer.*

King's Honeysuckle

This is distinguished from ordinary King's pattern by the additional decorative device which appears below the shell at the top of the stem (on the back with spoons and the front with forks).

It was first made for the service at Windsor, from about 1808 and onwards, which consists of over 2,000 pieces. Most of this pattern was produced in the 1820s and 1830s.

There are four variants (Figure 174): (1) Union shell heel. (2) Union shell heel (convex shell). (3) Anthemion or honeysuckle heel. (4) Husk heel.

Services can be found, and building a service would be possible but not easy.

See Figures 173 and 174.

Pitfalls

Confusion with King's and Queen's patterns.

Figure 173. *King's Honeysuckle pattern, Anthemion heel. Pair of dessert forks, London, 1822, Robert Peppin. Courtesy C.J. Vander.*

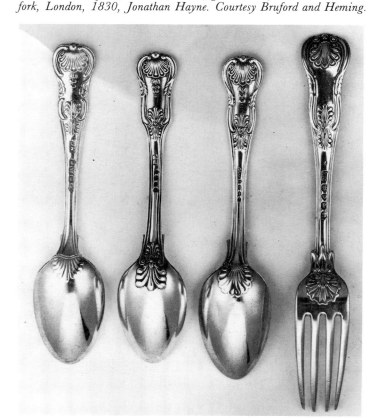

Figure 174. *King's Honeysuckle pattern, from left to right: convex Union shell heel. Teaspoon, London, 1834, Mary Chawner; Anthemion or Honeysuckle heel. Teaspoon, London, 1822, Robert Peppin; Union shell heel. Teaspoon, London, 1824, John Meek; husk heel. Dessert fork, London, 1830, Jonathan Hayne. Courtesy Bruford and Heming.*

Queen's or Rosette

An early nineteenth century pattern similar to, and often mistaken for, King's pattern. Queen's is in fact slightly heavier in appearance. The quickest point to look at is the shell at the top *front* of the stem which, with Queen's, is convex, i.e. standing out, whereas with standard King's it is concave (stamped in). Remember, however, that the shell on the top *back* of the stem is convex in both cases for the standard form.

This pattern appears in the Chawner & Co. Pattern Book not as Queen's, by which name it is best known today, but as Rosette.

It will be found both double and single struck and with variants of each.

Double struck in its standard form has an anthemion or honeysuckle heel. The more unusual form is with an oyster heel. Also, but very rare, is a convex Union shell heel.

Single struck is found either with shoulders (Chawner Pattern Book Rosette Front French Shoulder) or without (Chawner Pattern Book Rosette Front Round Handle). In both cases, not only is the back plain, but also the lower half of the front.

Queen's has been produced in quite large quantities from its introduction to the present day. Both straight and mixed services can be found relatively easily.

This is a good pattern for building a service.

See Figures 175-177.

Pitfalls

Condition is particularly important with a decorative pattern such as this.

Confusion between this and other similar patterns can be a problem (see for example Scroll Rosette, p. 127).

176

175

177

Figure 175. *Queen's pattern. Left, oyster back. Table spoon, London, 1828, Jonathan Hayne; right, standard pattern with anthemion or honeysuckle heel. Dessert fork (which has been in a fire), London, 1854, J. & H. Savory. Courtesy Bruford and Heming.*

Figure 176. *Modern examples of Queen's pattern. Courtesy C.J. Vander.*

Figure 177. *Scottish example of single struck Queen's pattern with shoulders. Teaspoon, Glasgow, 1866. Courtesy Bruford and Heming.*

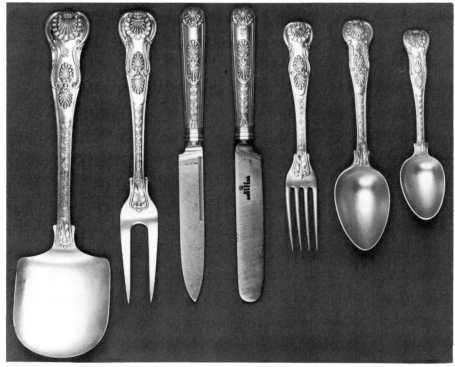

Figure 178. *Scroll Rosette pattern. Dessert spoons, London, 1822, Wms. Eley & Fearn. Courtesy C.J. Vander.*

Figure 179. *Paul Storr variant of King's pattern (Double Shell and Laurel). Examples from a silver-gilt dessert service for eighteen. London, 1811, mainly by Paul Storr. Courtesy James Charles.*

Figure 180. *King's variant with husk shells. Table forks, London, 1839, Mary Chawner. Courtesy Commercial Smelting Co.*

Figure 181. *Dolphin pattern dessert fork, London, 1860, Geo. W. Adams of Chawner & Co. Courtesy Commercial Smelting Co.*

Figure 182. *Princess No. 2. Dessert forks. Left, London 1884, Aldwinckle & Slater. Right, London, 1834, Mary Chawner. Courtesy Commercial Smelting Co.*

Figure 183. *King's variant (pattern of unknown name). Table spoons, London, 1825, Robert Garrard, and 1827, William Chawner. Courtesy Commercial Smelting Co.*

180   181   182   183

Scroll Rosette

A scarce variant of Queen's or Rosette pattern which appears in the Chawner & Co. Pattern Book.

There are two important features which distinguish this from ordinary Queen's or Rosette pattern. First, the leaf-work heel which is not found with Queen's; secondly the rosette one third the way down the stem. With this pattern the centre of the scrolls on either side are in line with the centre of the rosette (Figure 178); with Queen's the lower ends of the scrolls are in line with the centre of the rosette. The design of the rosette itself is also different (compare with Queen's pattern Figures 175-177).

Services exist but are scarce. Building a service would be difficult but possible.

Pitfalls

Confusion with Queen's pattern.

Double Shell and Laurel (see also King's Shape 'Laurel', p. 131)

This magnificent variant of King's pattern was produced, as might be expected, by Paul Storr. It incorporates a double shell at the top (convex and concave), a more elaborate honeysuckle device in the centre of the stem and laurel decoration on the lower stems (Figure 179).

A rare and very expensive pattern. Finding any pieces would be difficult; building a service probably impossible.

With Husk Shells (pattern of unknown name; for King's Husk see p. 136)

A Mary Chawner variant of King's pattern which combines elements of King's Husk and Scroll Rosette. The shells, back, front and heel, are of husk type. A four petal flower has been used on the front, with scrolls surrounding in a similar but less bold manner to Scroll Rosette.

Finding any pieces would be difficult; building a service probably impossible.
See Figure 180.

Dolphin

A rare Chawner & Co. pattern (Figure 181) of the basic form. Finding any pieces would be difficult; building a service probably impossible.

Princess No. 2

A rare nineteenth century pattern which appears in the Chawner & Co. Pattern Book.

Odd pieces may be found. Building a service would be very difficult.
See Figure 182.

Pattern of unknown name

An interesting early variant of King's with asymmetric leaf work replacing the shells, and the anthemion and scroll decoration replaced by formal shell work.

Pieces will only rarely be found; building a service would probably be impossible.
See Figure 183.

Bacchanalian

A rare Regency pattern designed by Stothard for Rundell Bridge & Rundell, the earliest pieces dating from 1812 in the Royal Collection. Most pieces are by Paul Storr and his successors, and in the first instance it appears to have been produced only for dessert services. The majority of pieces of this pattern are gilded.

The pattern is still made today.

It is very difficult to find any pieces of this pattern. Complete early dessert services are extremely rare, and it would be very difficult to build a nineteenth century dessert service. This is certainly not a pattern to collect other than for a dessert service, or unless you want a modern service based on an interesting early nineteenth century design.

See Figures 184 and 185.

Pitfalls

Since this pattern emanated from such an important workshop, beware of cast fakes.

184

185

Figure 184. *Chawner & Co. examples of Bacchanalian pattern. Silver-gilt table spoons, 1852 and 1870. Courtesy Sotheby's.*

Figure 185. *Part of a Bacchanalian pattern silver-gilt dessert service. London, 1890, Wakely & Wheeler. Courtesy Sotheby's.*

Boar Hunt and Mask

This is one of the patterns which, like Bacchanalian, was designed by Thomas Stothard for Rundell Bridge & Rundell and made by Paul Storr and his successors. (There is evidence to show that the modelling of the knives was carried out by Sir Francis Chantry, R.A.)

Over 1,300 pieces of this pattern were made for the Royal Collection between 1811 and 1814, but otherwise it is a rare pattern, and the chances of ever building a service are very remote.

See Figure 186.

Pitfalls

Cast fakes from original examples would be the greatest danger encountered.

Fox Hunt

A very rare pattern of the 1840s, essentially the same as the Stag Hunt (see below) with the exception of the animal being pursued. The back is the same.

No service is known to exist; building a service would be impossible.
See Figure 187.

Pitfalls

Confusion at a quick glance with Stag or Boar Hunt is a danger.

Stag Hunt

A very rare Regency pattern designed for Rundell Bridge & Rundell by Stothard and first made by Paul Storr. Examples can be found from later in the nineteenth century, mostly by Paul Storr's successors.

The pattern is still produced today, including a pierced version.

Building a nineteenth century service would be virtually impossible.
See Figures 188 and 189.

Pitfalls

Cast fakes from Paul Storr originals are the greatest danger.

Figure 186. *Boar Hunt and Mask pattern. Dessert spoon, London, 1822, Wms. Eley & Fearn. Courtesy Victoria and Albert Museum.*

Figure 188. *Stag Hunt pattern on a modern table fork. Courtesy C.J. Vander.*

Figure 187. *Fox Hunt pattern. A pair of sauce ladles. London, 1844, John and Henry Lias. Courtesy Sotheby's.*

Figure 189. *Stag Hunt pattern. Silver-gilt dessert pieces, London, 1831. Notice that a different die (reverse) has been used for the spoon and the fork. Courtesy Phillips.*

Old England

A very rare early nineteenth century pattern decorated with symbolic plants of the British Isles. With the earliest known examples dating from 1830 it is probable that this pattern was first produced for the coronation of William IV.

A service is known to exist; building a service would be almost impossible.

See Figure 190.

'Star and Cornucopia' (pattern of unknown name)

A very rare Lias Brothers pattern of King's Shape decorated with a star, cornucopia, shamrock and thistle on the front of the stem, and with sprays of oak and laurel, together with a shamrock and thistle, on the back. The heel is decorated with a star. Known examples were made in 1839/40.

From the symbolism present, it is probable that this pattern was inspired by some contemporary event such as Queen Victoria's coronation, or her marriage in 1840 to Prince Albert. (For a similar possibility see Old England pattern above.)

No service is known to exist; building a service would probably be impossible.

See Figure 191.

Figure 190. *Old England pattern. Fish slice, London, 1830. Private Collection.*

Figure 191. *King's Shape, 'Star and Cornucopia' pattern. Table fork, London, 1839, Lias Brothers. Courtesy Commercial Smelting Co.*

'Laurel' (pattern of unknown name)

A very rare nineteenth century pattern produced for Hunt & Roskell. It combines the King's Shape with formally arranged laurel leaves along the stem.

Finding any pieces would be very difficult; building a service would be almost impossible.

See Figure 192.

Rose

An early nineteenth century variant of the King's Shape, decorated with trailing roses, and still in production today (see die for teaspoon Figure 10).

Two types are known: (1) Anthemion or honeysuckle heel. This is the standard pattern today (see Figure 10). (2) Union shell heel. Mostly found on early examples (Figure 193).

Early pieces and services are rare. Building an early service would be very difficult.

Figure 192. *King's Shape 'Laurel'. Silver-gilt dessert spoon, London, 1850, Hunt & Roskell. Courtesy Victoria and Albert Museum.*

Figure 193. *Rose pattern with Union shell heel. Teaspoons, London, 1825, John, Henry and Charles Lias. Courtesy C.J. Vander.*

Figure 194. *Modern silver-gilt Bright Vine dessert fork (back) and soup spoon (front). Courtesy C.J. Vander.*

Figure 195. *King's Shape 'Trailing Vine' pattern. Table spoons, London, 1836, Samuel Hayne and Dudley Cater. Courtesy C.J. Vander.*

Bright Vine (see also King's Shape 'Trailing Vine' below)

A pattern first produced in the mid-nineteenth century and still in production today; it is listed in Chawner's Pattern Book as Bright Vine.

Essentially this is a later variation of the Hourglass/King's/Queen's group; while the shaping of the stems is identical, the shells and other decorative motives of the earlier patterns are replaced by vine leaves and grapes.

Services exist but are scarce. Building a service would be very difficult.

See Figure 194.

'Trailing Vine' (pattern of unknown name; see also Bright Vine above)

A very rare pattern combining the King's Shape with grapes and vines.

Odd pieces may occasionally be found. Building a service would probably be impossible.

See Figure 195.

Chased Vine (see also Pierced Vine below)

An early nineteenth century pattern of King's outline, produced principally for dessert services. Made intermittently up to the present day and still in production. The majority of examples are gilded.

Early nineteenth century dessert services exist but are scarce. Building anything but a dessert service of the nineteenth century would be impossible.

See Figures 196 and 197.

Pierced Vine (Chased and Pierced Vine)

A mid-nineteenth century variant of the Chased Vine pattern with pierced decoration (the King's Shape has almost disappeared in this version). Although mostly produced for dessert services, table pieces were also made. This pattern is still in production.

Services and pieces can be found; building a service, particularly dessert, would be possible but not easy.

See Figure 198.

Figure 196. *Chased Vine. Silver-gilt dessert service, London, 1831, William Eaton. Courtesy Sotheby's.*

Figure 197. *Chased Vine. Notice that the back of the spoon bowl is also decorated with vines. Examples from a mixed silver-gilt dessert service, London, c.1835/89, Theobald & Atkinson, Francis Higgins, Rawlings & Summers, F.W. Figg and William Traies. Courtesy Sotheby's.*

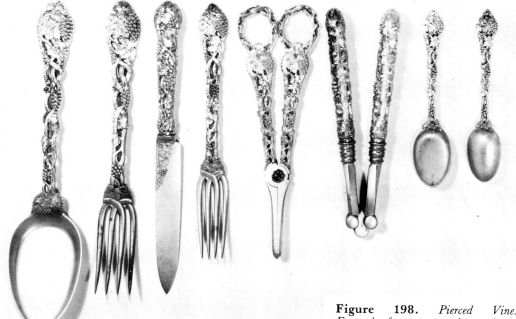

Figure 198. *Pierced Vine. Examples from an extensive service by Elkington. Courtesy Phillips.*

Coburg

Designed for Rundell Bridge & Rundell in about 1810, this rare pattern was made by Paul Storr and is perhaps the pattern for which he is best known. Storr's successors continued to produce examples and it is still made today. An oyster heel is usual (see Figure 175).

Complete nineteenth century services do exist but are rare. It would be possible, but very difficult, to build a service.

See frontispiece and Figure 199.

Pitfalls

Cast fakes of genuine Paul Storr examples are the greatest danger.

King's Shape 'Elizabethan' (pattern of unknown name)

This very rare pattern combines King's Shape with decoration very similar to the Elizabethan pattern (see p. 93). It is one of the patterns produced for Hunt & Roskell by George W. Adams of Chawner & Co.

The term King's Shape 'Elizabethan' is a recognisable description.

Odd pieces may occasionally be found. Building a service would be almost impossible.

See Figure 200.

Pitfalls

Confusion with Elizabethan.

200   **201**

Figure 200. *King's Shape 'Elizabethan'. Silver-gilt dessert spoon, London, 1870, Hunt & Roskell overstamping G.W. Adams of Chawner & Co. Teaspoon a pattern with the same maker's marks. Courtesy Victoria and Albert Museum.*

Figure 199. *Modern examples of the Coburg pattern. Courtesy C.J. Vander.*

Figure 201. *Plantagenet pattern. Table forks, London, 1875, Geo. W. Adams of Chawner & Co. Courtesy Commercial Smelting Co.*

Figure 202. *King's Shape 'Rococo', a pattern of unknown name. Examples from an extensive service, London, 1883, Francis Higgins, overstruck by Hunt & Roskell. Courtesy Sotheby's.*

Figure 203. *'Scottish King's Shape' (rococo end), a pattern of unknown name. Notice the use of a die for the crest (Cuninghame of Craigends, Co., Renfrew). Glasgow 1844/48, Robert Gray & Son. Courtesy Sotheby's.*

Plantagenet

A very rare mid-nineteenth century pattern which appears in the Chawner & Co. Pattern Book.

Odd examples may be found. Building a service would be extremely difficult.
See Figure 201.

Cambridge

A nineteenth century rococo variant of the King's Shape which appears in the Chawner & Co. Pattern Book (see p. 219).

Services and individual pieces are rare; building a service would be extremely difficult.

Not illustrated.

King's Shape 'Rococo' (pattern of unknown name)

A rare nineteenth century pattern produced for Hunt & Roskell by Francis Higgins.
Finding any pieces would be difficult; building a service probably impossible.
See Figure 202.

'Scottish King's Shape' (Rococo End) (pattern of unknown name)

A rare Scottish single struck decorated King's Shape variant with plain stem and no shoulders.

Finding pieces would be difficult; building a service probably impossible.
See Figure 203.

Pattern of Unknown Name

A late nineteenth century pattern whose King's Shape origins are evident.
Pieces are rare; building a service would probably be impossible.
See Figure 204.

King's Shape Double Threaded

A rare pattern listed in the Chawner & Co. Pattern Book.
Services exist but are rare. Building a service would be extremely difficult.
See Figure 205.

King's Husk

A variant of the King's pattern, the principal and most obvious difference being the omission of the central honeysuckle decoration on the stem. A husk shell also replaces the concave shell of King's pattern and there is no shell on the back.

It was first produced during the Regency and is still made today. Examples can be found by Paul Storr.

There are three principal types: (1) Husk heel (standard form). (2) Anthemion or honeysuckle heel. (3) Union Shell heel (rare).

In addition to the principal types, a number of variants can occasionally be found.

204   205   206

Figure 204. *A late nineteenth century pattern of unknown name. Table spoons, London, 1898, W. Hutton & Sons. Courtesy Commercial Smelting Co.*

Figure 205. *King's Shape Double Threaded. Part of a service. London, 1851/58, Geo. W. Adams of Chawner & Co. Courtesy Sotheby's.*

Figure 206. *King's Husk pattern. Left, husk heel. Dessert fork, London, 1838, Mary Chawner. Right, anthemion or honeysuckle heel. Dessert fork, London, 1838. Courtesy Bruford and Heming.*

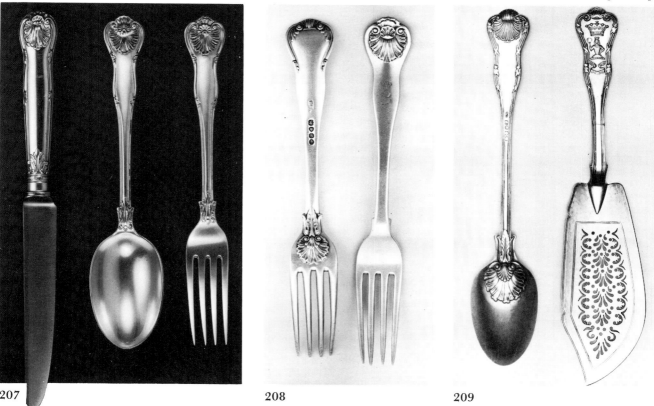

207   208   209

Figure 207. *Modern C.J. Vander examples of the King's Husk pattern. Courtesy C.J. Vander.*

Figure 208. *Plain Edge King's Husk, a rare variant. Table forks, one London, 1836, Mary Chawner; the other London, 1860, Hunt & Roskell. Courtesy Commercial Smelting Co.*

Figure 209. *Reverse King's Husk (reed and ribbon edge). Notice that the crest, motto and coronet (Earls of Kintore) have been die stamped. Fish slice and gravy spoon from a large service, London, 1849, Geo. W. Adams of Chawner & Co. Courtesy Sotheby's.*

Other variants are the very rare Reverse King's Husk, which has the husk shell on the back instead of the front of the stem (see Figure 209 for a variant of the reverse form). Also very rare is a variant with a 'Queen's' type shell replacing the husk shell on both the back and the front (not illustrated).

Services of standard form exist but are scarce. Building a service would be possible but not easy.

See Figures 206 and 207.

Plain Edge King's Husk

A variant with no edge decoration. Pieces are very rare; building a service would be impossible.

See Figure 208.

Reverse King's Husk (reed and ribbon edge; pattern of unknown name)

This rare variant with reed and ribbon edge also has the husk on the back instead of the front of the stem. This has been done in order that the crest (Earls of Kintore) could be stamped on the front.

See Figure 209.

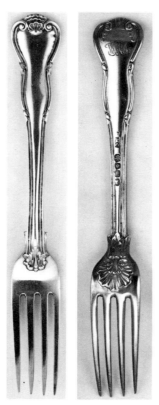

Figure 210. *King's Husk (without husk). This variant does not have the husk shell (see also Adelaide pattern). Dessert fork, London, 1838, Mary Chawner. Courtesy Bruford and Heming.*

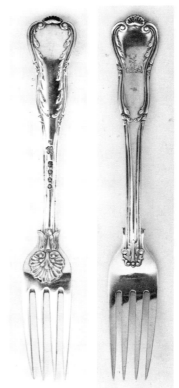

Figure 211. *Adelaide pattern. Dessert fork, London, 1885, J.A. & T.S. Courtesy C.J. Vander.*

210   211

King's Husk (without husk)

A very rare variant of King's Husk without the husk shell at the top front of the stem.

Odd pieces can be found; building a service would be almost impossible.
See Figure 210.

Adelaide

A very rare variant of King's Husk, lacking the husk shell at the top front of the stem and with the addition of leaf work to the edges.

Building a service would be almost impossible.
See Figure 211.

Pitfalls

Confusion with other King's Husk variants.

Princess No. 1

A nineteenth century pattern of similar but rather lighter form to the Albert pattern (p. 140).

Referred to today mostly as Princess, it appears in the Chawner & Co. Pattern Book as Princess No. 1.

It has been produced intermittently up to the present day.

Services exist but are scarce; building a service would be difficult but possible.
See Figures 212 and 213.

Pitfalls

Confusion between the heavier Albert, the lighter Marie, and some of the King's Husk variants could be a problem when purchasing an individual example. Carry a sample with you if you are building a service.

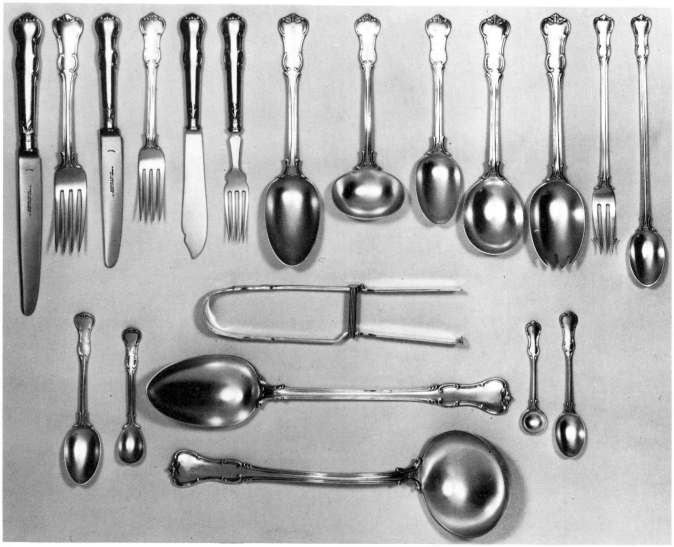

Figure 212. *Princess No. 1 pattern. Samples from an extensive service. London, the majority 1859/77, by Geo. W. Adams of Chawner & Co. Courtesy Phillips.*

Figure 213. *Modern examples of C.J. Vander Princess No. 1 pattern. Courtesy C.J. Vander.*

214

215

Figure 214. *Devonshire pattern. A pair of dessert forks, London, 1849, Geo. W. Adams of Chawner & Co. Courtesy C.J. Vander.*

Figure 215. *The two principal types of Albert pattern. Left, leaf scroll heel. Right, thread heel. Courtesy Bruford and Heming.*

Figure 216. *Modern examples of Albert pattern. Courtesy C.J. Vander.*

Devonshire

A rare mid-nineteenth century pattern similar to Albert and Princess No. 1. Pieces can be found but not easily; building a service would be very difficult.
See Figure 214.

Pitfalls

Confusion with Princess No. 1 and Albert patterns, both of which it closely resembles.

Albert and Classic

This is a scarce pattern of the mid-nineteenth century named after Prince Albert. It was first used in about 1840 (the year of Prince Albert's marriage to Queen Victoria) and is still produced today. The design is one of the mid-Victorian rococo revival forms, being one of the shaped decorative variants of Fiddle pattern.

There are three variations of this pattern:

(1) Albert with thread heel. (2) Albert with leaf scroll heel. (3) Classic pattern, which is listed in Chawner's Pattern Book as a separate pattern, but is essentially Albert with a plain stem and shoulders.

Of the three variants the thread heel is the most common, and Classic, which is usually single struck, the most rare.

Complete services may be found, and it is possible to build a service.
See Figures 215 and 216.

Pitfalls

No special traps with this pattern other than perhaps mistaking it for the more simple Princess No. 1 pattern or with Devonshire and Victoria.

Victoria (see also Albert pattern)

A pattern named, quite naturally, after Queen Victoria and of similar, but more angular, design to the Albert pattern.

It was first produced around 1840 and then intermittently through the nineteenth century.

Services exist but are rare; building a service would be difficult but possible.

See Figures 217 and 218.

Pitfalls

When building a service confusion with both the Albert and Devonshire patterns is the greatest danger. Always carry a sample with you.

Figure 217. *Victoria pattern. Dessert forks, London, 1840. Courtesy Phillips.*

Figure 218. *Victoria pattern. Examples from a large service, London, 1854, Henry Holland. Courtesy Sotheby's.*

Mid- and Late Nineteenth Century

(in alphabetical order; patterns of unknown names at end)

Some patterns of this period have been included in other sections, particularly those of King's Shape.

See also the following section, Arts and Crafts, etc.

Albany (also known as Queen Anne)

A pattern of the nineteenth century first used in the mid-1880s and appearing in the Francis Higgins catalogue as Queen Anne. It is largely a variant of the Onslow pattern of the eighteenth century. Its peak of popularity was at the turn of the century and it is still produced today, although not in large quantities.

Complete services can be found and are generally in good condition. Building a service would be fairly straightforward.

See Figures 219 and 338.

Pitfalls

There are no special pitfalls with this pattern. It should not be confused with the Onslow pattern (see Onslow pattern, p. 172) which it resembles.

Figure 219. *Modern examples of Albany pattern. Courtesy C.J. Vander.*

Beaded Knurled (see p. 220)

A rare pattern of the second half of the nineteenth century which appears in the Chawner & Co. Pattern Book. It has the some outline as the Fern pattern, i.e. pointed end (see Figure 221). The stem is plain and, as its name implies, it has a gadrooned and beaded edge (gadrooning on the outside).

Any pieces are rare; building a service would be extremely difficult.

Not illustrated.

Figure 220. *Canova pattern. These examples are from an electro-gilt service of the mid-nineteenth century. Courtesy Sotheby's.*

Canova

This pattern was first produced in about 1850 and exhibited by Chawner & Co. at the Great Exhibition in 1851, being based on Canova's 'Hebe', 'Sappho' and the 'Dancing Girl Reposing'.

It appears to have been produced only for dessert services and even these are very rare.

Building anything but a dessert service would be impossible and even this would be difficult.

See Figure 220.

Empire

A French inspired pattern which appears in the Francis Higgins Pattern Book. It is similar to Hunt & Roskell's Louis XV (p. 146) but is more elaborate, with a shell replacing the leaf work at the top and no plain surface left for a crest on the front.

Not illustrated.

Figure 221. *Fern pattern. Part of an extensive table and dessert service, London, 1876 by Geo. W. Adams of Chawner & Co. Courtesy Christie's.*

Fern

A rare mid-nineteenth century Chawner & Co. pattern, illustrated in their Pattern Book, showing the influence of naturalism.

Any examples are difficult to find; building a service would be almost impossible. See Figure 221.

Georgian (B) (also known as Queen Anne)

A late nineteenth century pattern, a cross between Dog Nose and Hanoverian, which is still in production. The decoration at the end of the stem matches the so-called Queen Anne tea and coffee services of the late nineteenth/early twentieth centuries.

Services are not too difficult to find, and building a service would be possible. See Figure 222.

Grecian

A mid-nineteenth century pattern exhibited by Geo. W. Adams at the Great Exhibition and listed in the Chawner & Co. Pattern Book. Both double and single struck may be found.

Services can be found, and building a service would be possible. See Figure 223.

Italian (Registered Italian)

A rare late nineteenth century pattern illustrated by Francis Higgins in his Pattern Book. Its design is basically pointed end, with formal foliate scroll work on the stem and a pellet at the top.

Not illustrated.

Figure 222. *Georgian (B) or Queen Anne pattern. Part of an extensive service by Elkington, Birmingham, 1900. Courtesy Sotheby's.*

Figure 223. *Grecian pattern. Part of a mixed service by Aldwinckle & Slater, 1884/86, and Chawner & Co., 1869. The spoon on the right is from a Chawner & Co. service, 1860/76. Courtesy Sotheby's.*

Lily

The Lily pattern was first produced in 1850, the design being registered in that year by Elkington. It appears in the Chawner & Co. Pattern Book as Lily. This style is a good example of mid-Victorian naturalism.

Services exist but are scarce; building a service would be possible.

See Figure 224.

Louis XV

A pattern of very obvious French inspiration produced for Hunt & Roskell in the mid-nineteenth century.

As with all Hunt & Roskell flatware the quality is superb.

Finding any pieces would be difficult; building a service would be extremely difficult.

See Figure 225.

Napier

The design for this rare Chawner & Co. pattern was registered on 10th January, 1862 and appears in their Pattern Book.

Odd pieces may be found, but building a service would be extremely difficult.

See Figure 226.

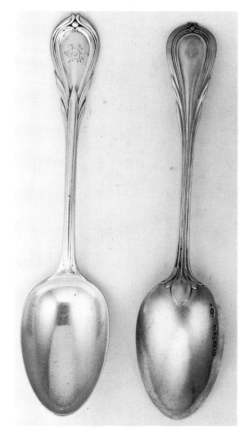

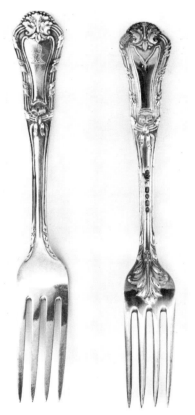

Figure 224. *Lily pattern. Pair of dessert spoons, London, 1879, Geo. W. Adams of Chawner & Co. Courtesy C.J. Vander.*

Figure 225. *Louis XV pattern. Dessert forks, London, 1856, Hunt & Roskell overstamping another, probably Geo. W. Adams of Chawner & Co. Courtesy Commercial Smelting Co.*

Figure 226. *Napier pattern. Table fork, London, 1862; dessert spoon, London, 1867. Both by Geo. W. Adams of Chawner & Co. Courtesy Commercial Smelting Co.*

New Gothic

A rare Chawner & Co. pattern, the design for which was registered December 13th, 1854 and which appears in their Pattern Book.

Odd pieces may be found; building a service would be extremely difficult.
See Figure 227.

Newton (see p. 220)

A very rare pattern which appears in the Chawner & Co. Pattern Book.

Of Hanoverian form the stem is decorated (back and front) with foliate scrolls of similar form to those found on engraved Trefids (see Figure 76). The top of the stem is decorated on the front with an anthemion, the central lobe of which is extended within a plain reserve which points down the stem. The heel is an anthemion within beading.

Finding any pieces is extremely difficult.

Not illustrated.

Ornamental Elizabethan

A rare mid-nineteenth century pattern incorporating Renaissance and later decorative motifs.

The design was registered 21st December, 1852 and was produced by Francis Higgins for Hunt & Roskell.

Odd examples may be found; building a service would be very difficult.
See Figure 228.

Figure 227. *New Gothic pattern. Pair of table spoons, London, 1856, Geo. W. Adams of Chawner & Co. Courtesy Commercial Smelting Co.*

Figure 228. *Ornamental Elizabethan pattern. Table fork, London, 1871, Francis Higgins. Courtesy Commercial Smelting Co.*

Palm

A very rare mid-nineteenth century pattern produced by Chawner & Co. in whose Pattern Book it appears.

Services are known to exist, but are very rare. Odd pieces may be found, but building a service would be extremely difficult.

See Figures 229 and 230.

Paxton

A very rare mid-nineteenth century pattern, named after Joseph Paxton the designer of the Crystal Palace for the Great Exhibition.

It is illustrated in the Chawner & Co. Pattern Book.

Services are very rare. Odd pieces may be found, but building a service would be extremely difficult.

See Figure 231.

Registered Italian (see Italian (Registered) p. 144).

Rich Bead (Prince of Wales)

A late nineteenth century machine-made Elkington pattern which appears in their catalogue. It also appears in John Round's catalogue of c.1900, where the name is given as 'Prince of Wales'.

Services can be found, although not easily, while building a service would be possible but difficult.

See Figure 232.

Rich Figure

A rare pattern of the second half of the nineteenth century, which appears in the Francis Higgins Pattern Book and was made by him for Hunt & Roskell.

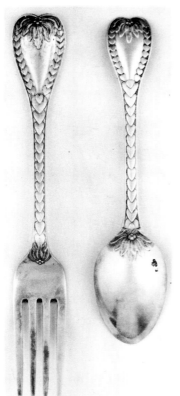

Figure 229. *Palm pattern. Casting of a knife shaft. Courtesy Bruford and Heming.*

Figure 230. *Palm pattern. Dessert fork and teaspoon. Hunt & Roskell patterns. Courtesy Victoria and Albert Museum.*

Figure 231. *Paxton pattern. Table fork, London, 1868, Geo. W. Adams of Chawner & Co. Courtesy Victoria and Albert Museum.*

229

230

231

Figure 232. *Rich Bead pattern. Left, table spoon, Sheffield, 1899, J. Round. Right, table fork, Birmingham, 1892, Elkington. Courtesy Commercial Smelting Co.*

Figure 233. *Rich Figure pattern. Table and dessert fork with a table knife. Francis Higgins patterns. Notice that the blade of the knife is stamped Hunt & Roskell. Courtesy Victoria and Albert Museum.*

Figure 234. *Straight Tudor pattern. Dessert forks, London, 1851, Geo. W. Adams of Chawner & Co. Courtesy Commercial Smelting Co.*

Odd pieces may be found on rare occasions; building a service would probably be impossible.

See Figure 233.

Tamworth (see p. 219)

A rare mid-nineteenth century pattern which appears in the Chawner & Co. Pattern Book. It has a moulded edge with a leaf in the moulding at each side of the rounded end and delicate formal scroll work between. The heel comprises three-leaf scrolls.

Any pieces are very difficult to find.

Not illustrated.

Straight Tudor (see also Tudor, p. 150)

A rare nineteenth century Chawner & Co. design which appears in their Pattern Book.

It was registered, along with Tudor, on 14th August, 1850.

Services and pieces are rare; building a service would be extremely difficult.

Pitfalls

Confusion with Tudor which has a small scroll projecting from each side of the stem about a third of the way down from the top.

See Figure 234.

Tudor (see also Straight Tudor, p. 149)

A rare Chawner & Co. pattern registered August 14th, 1850 along with straight Tudor. It appears in Chawner's Pattern Book.

Services as well as odd pieces may, on rare occasions, be found, but building a service would be extremely difficult.

Pitfalls

Confusion with Straight Tudor which does not have the small projections from the stem.

See Figure 235.

Wellington

A scarce mid-nineteenth century pattern named after the Great Duke. It appears in the Chawner & Co. Pattern Book, and is still produced today.

Two types are known: (1) With a double thread down the length of the stem ending at the bowl with scrolls (as appears in the Pattern Book). (2) With plain lower half of the stem.

Services and pieces may be found but are scarce; building a service would be possible but difficult.

See Figures 236 and 237.

235

236

237

Figure 235. *Tudor pattern. Teaspoon with design registration mark for August 14th, 1850. Mark of Hunt & Roskell overstamping Geo. W. Adams of Chawner & Co. Courtesy Victoria and Albert Museum.*

Figure 236. *Wellington pattern 1. Examples from an extensive service, Sheffield, 1909/10, James Dixon & Sons. Courtesy Sotheby's.*

Figure 237. *Wellington pattern 2. London, 1855/57, Geo. W. Adams of Chawner & Co. Courtesy Sotheby's.*

238   239   240

Figure 238. *Wellington variant. Table spoon, London, 1850, Geo. W. Adams of Chawner & Co. Courtesy Commercial Smelting Co.*

Figure 239. *Pattern of unknown name. Dessert spoon and fork, London, 1853, SH. DC. Courtesy Bourdon-Smith.*

Figure 240. *Pattern of unknown name (Hunt & Roskell Rococo). Table spoon and fork, London, 1857, Hunt & Roskell overstamping Geo. W. Adams of Chawner & Co. Courtesy C.J. Vander.*

Wellington Variant (pattern of unknown name)

Found in the mid-nineteenth century this appears to have been a variant produced by Chawner & Co. for Hunt & Roskell.

Notice that the cartouche is asymmetric and that there are three leaves at its base, unlike the true Wellington pattern opposite.

Pieces are rare; building a service would be very difficult.

See Figure 238.

Pattern of Unknown Name

A French-inspired mid-nineteenth century pattern, the design for which was registered in 1852. Many features are similar to the Albert pattern (p. 140).

Pieces are rare; building a service would probably be impossible.

See Figure 239.

Pattern of Unknown Name (Hunt & Roskell Rococo)

This is one of the patterns produced specially for Hunt & Roskell in the mid-nineteenth century by Chawner and Higgins.

Pieces are rare; building a service would be very difficult.

See Figure 240.

Figure 241. *Lias Brothers pattern of unknown name. Table forks, London 1851 and 1858. Courtesy Commercial Smelting Co.*

Figure 242. *Holly-decorated pattern of unknown name. Dessert spoon and fork, London, 1892, EM. Courtesy Commercial Smelting Co.*

241

242

Pattern of Unknown Name (Lias Brothers)

A mid-nineteenth century pattern, by the Lias Brothers, of an overall form similar to the Dog Nose.

Pieces are rare; building a service would be very difficult.

See Figure 241.

Pattern of Unknown Name (holly-decorated)

A late nineteenth century pattern, probably with a name like Trailing Holly.

Pieces are very rare; building a service would probably be impossible.

See Figure 242.

Arts and Crafts
Aesthetic Movement
Art Nouveau and Allied Patterns

Aesthetic Movement
Ashbee, C.R. and the Guild of Handicrafts
Burges, William
Dresser, Dr. Christopher
Liberty (Knox, Archibald)
Mackintosh, Charles Rennie
Ramsden, Omar, & Carr, Alwyn

Aesthetic Movement

The opening of Japan to the West in the mid-nineteenth century led to a tremendous rash of Japanese influenced designs in the 1870s and 1880s.

In flatware this influence is mostly found with serving pieces and with tea and coffee spoons.

See Figures 243 and 244.

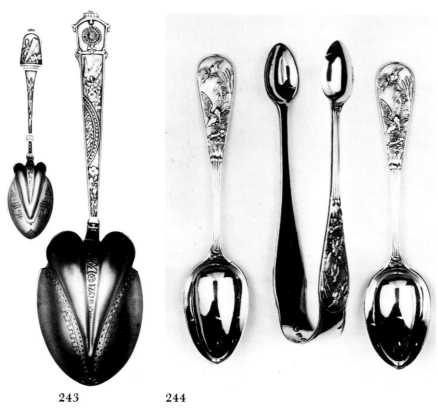

243   **244**

Figure 243. *Aesthetic Movement frosted and parcel-gilt serving spoon and ice cream spoon. London, 1875/6, Edward Barnard. Courtesy Sotheby's.*

Figure 244. *Part of a set of twelve silver-gilt Aesthetic Movement teaspoons and a pair of sugar tongs. London, 1882 by Holland Aldwinckle & Slater. Courtesy Sotheby's.*

C.R. Ashbee and the Guild of Handicrafts

The Guild of Handicrafts under C.R. Ashbee produced a number of mostly small serving pieces during its short existence (1887-1908). The use of cabochon stones can be seen in all the pieces. A clever use of wirework is often found in Ashbee designs and, in the case of flatware, this is mostly found with his knife hafts (Figure 245).

The most common pieces are the spoons made for use with his loop-handled dishes (Figure 246). Other pieces, such as teaspoons (Figure 247), are extremely rare.

Figure 245. *A Guild of Handicrafts Ltd. butter knife. London, 1900, the design attributed to C.R. Ashbee. Courtesy Sotheby's Belgravia.*

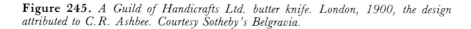

Figure 246. *A Guild of Handicrafts Ltd. spoon. London, 1905, designed by C.R. Ashbee. This type of spoon was for use with his loop-handled dishes or bowls. Courtesy Sotheby's Belgravia.*

Figure 247. *Three from a set of twelve very rare Guild of Handicrafts Ltd. coffee spoons. London, 1906. Notice the hammer marks left in the stem, a deliberate feature of Arts and Crafts pieces to indicate they were hand made. Courtesy Sotheby's Belgravia.*

William Burges

The architect William Burges (1827-81) designed a small number of pieces of flatware. All known examples show strong historicism. The set of spoons designed by Burges in the Victoria and Albert Museum is a mixture of Roman (with bowl, stem and keel) and Gothic form (the stem formed as a cluster column).

None of Burges' flatware designs was intended to be produced on any scale. They all must be regarded as 'one offs' resulting from individual commissions and pieces produced for personal use. The illustrated sugar tongs are almost certainly the latter (Figure 248).

Figure 248. *Sugar tongs engraved Willielmus Burges. London, 1870, Jes. Barkentin for Barkentin & Krall, approx. 4⅜ ins. long. The construction is unusual with a piece of wrought iron inlaid with gold being set into the sprung end. Courtesy Phillips.*

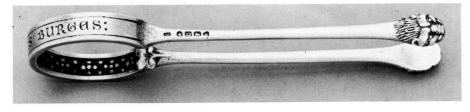

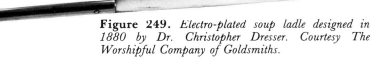

Figure 249. *Electro-plated soup ladle designed in 1880 by Dr. Christopher Dresser. Courtesy The Worshipful Company of Goldsmiths.*

Dr. Christopher Dresser

Dr. Dresser must be regarded as one of the most revolutionary designers of the nineteenth century. Functionalism and the economic use of material were two important aspects of his work. Decoration was a secondary consideration, used only to emphasise form or construction.

His most important metalwork designs were produced in the late 1870s and early 1880s, all of which were intended for mass-production and most of which were to be electro-plated.

The illustrated electro-plated soup ladle (Figure 249) designed *en suite* with a tureen, is an excellent example of Dr. Dresser's uncompromising design. It bears the design registration mark for 28th July, 1880.

Liberty

A range of Art Nouveau flatware was produced by Liberty. The most famous, Cymric, was designed by Archibald Knox in the late nineteenth century as part of a series which included such things as candlesticks, caskets and claret jugs.

Most examples found will be tea, coffee or caddy spoons, together with some coronation souvenir spoons. The most sought-after examples are those incorporating enamel decoration.

No service is known to exist; building a service would be impossible.

See Figures 250-255.

Pitfalls

Damage to the enamel is the only serious pitfall. Make sure also that there are no splits in any pierced or openwork.

250

251

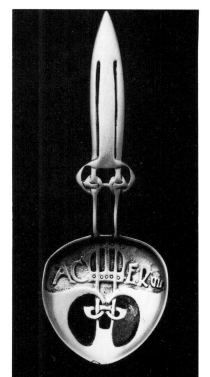

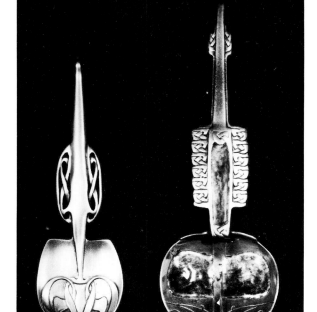

Figure 250. *Liberty & Co. Archibald Knox, Cymric coronation spoon with enamel in the bowl. Birmingham, 1901, with Rd. number 391475. Courtesy Sotheby's Belgravia.*

Figure 251. *Liberty & Co. Archibald Knox, Cymric. Left, Birmingham, 1902, with Rd. number 391477; right, Birmingham, 1901, with Rd. number 391478. Both these designs were used for coronation spoons; notice the use of enamel in the bowl of the spoon on the right. Courtesy Sotheby's Belgravia.*

252

253

Figure 252. *Liberty & Co. Three from a set of six Archibald Knox designed Cymric spoons with enamelled tops. Birmingham, 1903. Courtesy Sotheby's Belgravia.*

Figure 253. *Liberty & Co. One of a pair of serving spoons. London, 1899. Courtesy Sotheby's Belgravia.*

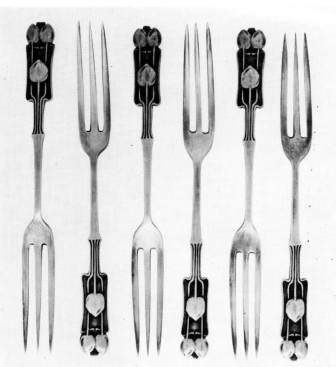

Figure 254. *Liberty & Co. Set of six pastry forks with enamel ends. Birmingham, 1923. Courtesy Sotheby's Belgravia.*

Figure 255. *Liberty & Co. Three from a set of six teaspoons with enamel ends. Birmingham, 1925. Courtesy Sotheby's Belgravia.*

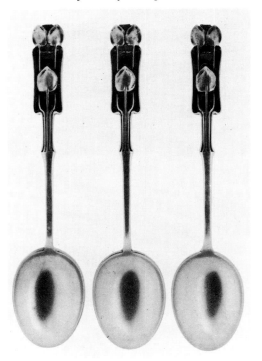

Charles Rennie Mackintosh

A few pieces of flatware can be found designed in 1903 by Mackintosh for the famous Ingram Street Tearooms which he designed for Miss Cranston. These are always electro-plated and are stamped 'Miss Cranston's'.

Two designs are found — Trefid and Trefoil. The most surprising aspect of both is their singular lack of originality. The Trefid, in particular, is a fairly straight copy of the original (see pp. 74-9).

Odd pieces can be found and are much sought after by collectors of Mackintosh.
See Figures 256-258.

Figure 256. *C.R. Mackintosh. Electro-plated fish knife and two spoons designed for the Ingram Street Tearooms, stamped 'Miss Cranston's'. Left and centre, Trefid; right, Trefoil. Courtesy Sotheby's Belgravia.*

Figure 258. *C.R. Mackintosh. Electro-plated 'Trefoil' tea and preserve spoons stamped 'Miss Cranston's'. Courtesy Sotheby's Belgravia.*

Figure 257. *C.R. Mackintosh. Electro-plated 'Trefid' spoon and forks stamped 'Miss Cranston's'. Courtesy Sotheby's Belgravia.*

Omar Ramsden & Alwyn Carr

A number of designs were produced both by the Ramsden & Carr partnership and, after its dissolution in 1919, by Ramsden on his own.

Although some historicism is found, most of the spoons show a fresh approach to flatware design.

Flatware was only a small part of the workshop's output, most of the production being confined to individual and cased sets of spoons as well as serving pieces.

Few services were ever produced. Building a service would be difficult if not impossible since few forks were made. Collecting is probably best confined to examples of the different designs.

See Figure 259.

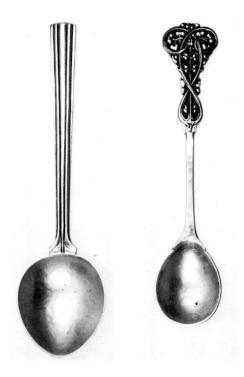

Figure 259. *Left, Omar Ramsden. Ribbed or reeded straight-handled spoon (with rat tail), London, 1929; right, Ramsden & Carr. Spoon decorated with leaf work and tendrils, London, 1910. Courtesy Phillips.*

Twentieth Century, c.1900-1950

(in alphabetical order; for Arts and Crafts and Art Nouveau see previous section)

This section gives only a cross section of the hundreds of patterns produced during this period, and is intended to give an impression of the sort of designs that were, and in many cases still are, in production.

The vast majority of patterns during this period were machine-made in Sheffield. Retailers would often commission 'exclusive' designs which make the problem of putting names to some of these patterns no easier.

Earlier designs, which continued to be produced, or were revived during this period, will be found in their relevant sections.

Beverley

A twentieth century machine-made Art Deco pattern which was most popular in the 1930s. Both services and parts of services (mostly teaspoons) are now coming on to the secondhand market.

Beverley is no longer produced so building a service would be difficult. Purchasing a complete service would be the most sensible approach.

See Figure 260.

Pitfalls

There were a number of services of similar design produced from about 1925 onwards with each manufacturer of the period having his own Art Deco pattern. If, therefore, you are trying to complete a service, it would be best to carry a sample or two with you to ensure a proper match.

Charles Boyton (Art Deco)

The illustrated Art Deco designed flatware (Figure 261) was made and signed by Charles Boyton in the 1930s. The earliest silversmith member of the Boyton family was another Charles, a spoon maker of the second quarter of the nineteenth century, whose apprenticeship pedigree may be traced back to Ebenezer Coker.

Chippendale

There are half a dozen or so mid-twentieth century patterns of this name, all of which appear to have been made in Sheffield.

See Figure 262.

Figure 260. *Beverley pattern. An Art Deco design of 1930s. Courtesy C.J. Vander.*

Figure 261. *Art Deco flatware by Charles Boyton. Courtesy M. McAleer.*

Figure 262. *Elkington Chippendale pattern. Courtesy Sotheby's.*

260

261

262

Dunstan

The name of this Art Deco pattern of the second quarter of the twentieth century is derived from the name of the patron saint of English goldsmiths, who lived during the mid-tenth century. There are strong similarities in stem shape to Puritan spoons of the mid-seventeenth century. The pattern, which was hand-made, is no longer produced.

Services are now starting to appear on the secondhand market. Most remain fairly complete, therefore building a service would be difficult.

See Figure 263.

Pitfalls

The only problem would be matching pieces properly when building or completing a service, although building a service at the present time is not advised.

'Georgian' (A)

Although given the name 'Georgian' this is a twentieth century interpretation of mid-eighteenth century forms. The pattern, which is hand-made, is based to the greatest extent on fancy back Hanoverian of about 1760. The tops are pointed rather than rounded, pointed ends being characteristic of late eighteenth century Irish and Scottish flatware. The fork has four prongs as with Old English, rather than the three prongs of the Hanoverian pattern.

'Georgian', is, therefore, not a bad name since this modern pattern is derived from the principal flatware patterns of the eighteenth century.

Most services produced in this pattern are still together, therefore finding odd secondhand examples to build a service would be difficult, and the collector would probably be wiser to purchase a complete service. As the pattern is still in production any missing pieces from a secondhand service could be replaced with new.

See Figure 264.

Lotus

First produced in the early twentieth century, this machine-made pattern derives its name from the Lotus motif which appears on the ends of the stems and hafts. The pattern is still in production today.

Services exist but are scarce, so building a service would be difficult.

See Figure 265.

Louis XIV

A similar but lighter pattern to Louis XV (see Figure 225) with a small shell instead of leaf work at the top. It is machine-made in Sheffield by Roberts & Belk.

Not illustrated.

Louis XVI

A similar pattern to Marie (see Figure 266), but with straight sides to the stem and a small shell at the top instead of the flower head. Machine-made in Sheffield by Roberts & Belk.

A slightly less decorated version with leaf work at the end and more pointed ends is produced by Mappin & Webb.

See also Figure 9 in the introduction.

Marie

A hand-made pattern produced in England in the twentieth century. Based on

263   264

Figure 263. *Dunstan pattern of the 1920s. Courtesy C.J. Vander.*

Figure 264. *'Georgian' (A) pattern. Courtesy C.J. Vander.*

Figure 265. *Lotus pattern. Courtesy C.J. Vander.*

Figure 266. *Marie pattern. Courtesy C.J. Vander.*

265   266

earlier French designs, it is still in production.

Secondhand services can be found. Most services are still intact, therefore odd pieces, other than tea and coffee spoons, are difficult to find. Building a service would be difficult.

See Figure 266.

Pitfalls

It would be possible, seeing examples in isolation, to confuse this pattern with the earlier Princess pattern.

Sandringham

A Viners pattern, machine-made in Sheffield. Gainsborough by Roberts & Belk is almost identical but has small scrolls at the base of the handle.
See Figure 267.

Windsor

A mid-twentieth century pattern produced by both Atkin Bros. and Roberts & Belk.
See Figure 268.

Figure 267. *Sandringham. Examples from an extensive service, Sheffield 1949/51, Viners. (Gainsborough by Roberts & Belk has scrolls at the base of the handle.) Courtesy Sotheby's.*

Figure 268. *Windsor pattern, all-silver cheese scoop, Sheffield, 1935, Atkin Bros. Courtesy M. McAleer.*

Figure 269. *Flatware by Gerald Benney. Courtesy the Worshipful Company of Goldsmiths.*

Twentieth Century, 1950-1980
(earlier designs still in production will be found in their relevant sections)

Benney, Gerald
Devlin, Stuart
Mellor, David
Vander, C.J.
Cutlery of the Eighties

Gerald Benney

For some years now Gerald Benney has ranked as one of the leading goldsmiths in the world. To him must be attributed the present day vogue for textured surfaces which is well illustrated by examples of his flatware from the mid-1960s.

See Figure 269.

Stuart Devlin

Stuart Devlin, who today ranks among the leading goldsmiths in the world, has designed several flatware patterns which are at present in production.

All reflect the functional aspects of modern design combined with textured and gilded surfaces which emphasise the richness of the metals from which they are produced. The patterns are unusual amongst modern flatware since they are entirely hand-forged.

Richard Cook (p.34 and Figure 18) is the master spoon maker responsible for all the flatware produced in Stuart Devlin's workshop since 1968.

Both services and part services are available.

See Figures 270-281.

Figure 270. *Arrow pattern by Stuart Devlin. Courtesy Stuart Devlin.*

Figure 271. *Champagne pattern by Stuart Devlin. Courtesy Stuart Devlin.*

Figure 272. *Diamond pattern by Stuart Devlin. Courtesy Stuart Devlin.*

Figure 273. *Feather pattern by Stuart Devlin. Courtesy Stuart Devlin.*

Figure 274. *Flare pattern by Stuart Devlin. Courtesy Stuart Devlin.*

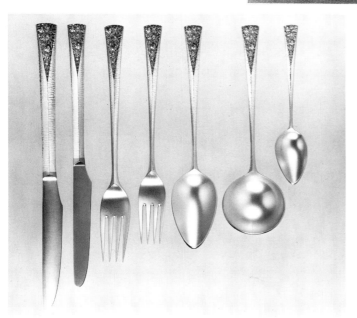

Figure 275. *Flower pattern by Stuart Devlin. Courtesy Stuart Devlin.*

Figure 276. *Parallel pattern by Stuart Devlin. Courtesy Stuart Devlin.*

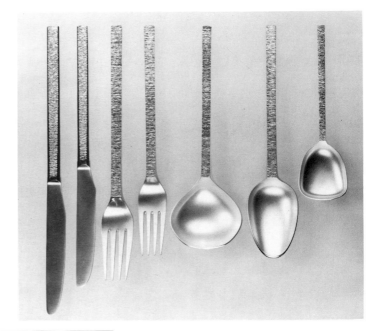

Figure 277. *Round-handled pattern by Stuart Devlin. Courtesy Stuart Devlin.*

Figure 278. *Square pattern by Stuart Devlin. Designed in 1981, this pattern has been limited to a production of twenty-five services, the size and range of each service depending on the choice of the individual clients. Courtesy Stuart Devlin.*

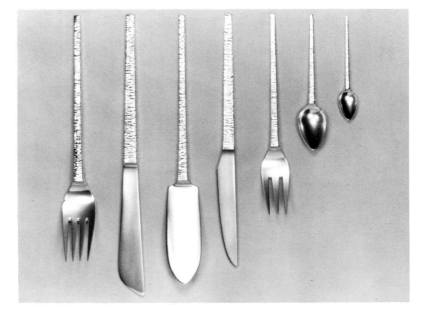

Figure 279. *Tetra-hedron pattern by Stuart Devlin. Courtesy Stuart Devlin.*

Figure 280. *Sauce, punch and soup ladles by Stuart Devlin. Courtesy Stuart Devlin.*

Figure 281. *Carving knife and fork by Stuart Devlin. Courtesy Stuart Devlin.*

Figure 282. *The Embassy pattern designed in the mid-1960s by David Mellor. Courtesy the Worshipful Company of Goldsmiths.*

David Mellor

One of the leading modern goldsmiths, David Mellor was commissioned in the 1960s to produce a new flatware pattern for use in British embassies throughout the world. After production had started the Government of the day, in an effort to curb public spending, cancelled the order. As a result this pattern has been made available for private use.

See Figure 282.

C.J. Vander

C.J. Vander is, for flatware, the natural successor of Chawner & Co., through Francis Higgins. Apart from continuing to make traditional patterns by hand the firm has also produced some completely modern designs.

See Figures 283-285.

Cutlery of the Eighties (prize winning design)

During 1980 M. Perovetz of London held a competition, in conjunction with the 'Loot' exhibition at Goldsmiths' Hall. The competition, for a new design, was open to anyone under the age of thirty, and over four hundred entries were submitted from which the winning design was selected.

The winner, Andrew Robinson was, at the time, a student at Sir John Cass College of Art in London, and his own comments on his approach to the design are worth quoting: ''It seemed obvious that any design which hoped to be a candidate for the Cutlery of the Eighties must be a design of our time and not simply a reflection of a previous era. After drawing up a number of preliminary ideas it became clear to me that the only way I would achieve my design objective was to start with the practical requirements of cutlery. This led me seriously to consider the most efficient shapes. At this point things began to fall into place and I found the cutlery really started to design itself. During my time at college I have often heard the design theory which says if you can get an article to function efficiently the aesthetic values will more or less take care of themselves. This certainly proved to be the case with my design.''

See Figure 286.

283

284

285

Figure 283. *A modern C.J. Vander pattern, with bark textured handles, currently in production. Courtesy C.J. Vander.*

Figure 284. *Coral, a modern C.J. Vander pattern, with heavily textured handles, currently in production. Courtesy C.J. Vander.*

Figure 285. *Mosaic, a modern C.J. Vander pattern, deriving its name from the mosaic effect given by its texturing. In current production. Courtesy C.J. Vander.*

Figure 286. *Cutlery of the Eighties, the winning design by Andrew Robinson. Courtesy H. Perovetz.*

Other Patterns or Groups

(patterns or groups not fitting into the previous sections)

'Bacchanals' (pattern of unknown name)
Historicism
Onslow or Scroll
Pierced-handle Flatware (other than standard patterns)
Private Dies
Tea and Coffee Spoons (other than standard patterns)
Whip

'Bacchanals' (pattern of unknown name; for Bacchanalian pattern see pp. 127-8)

A Regency pattern, in which the handles are formed as cast figures of Bacchanals with arms raised supporting baskets on their heads. The pattern was produced by Edward Farrell for dessert services, the earliest known examples being 1816.

Building any service other than dessert would not be possible since only dessert knives, forks, spoons and serving pieces are known.

Building a dessert service in itself would be very difficult.

See Figures 287 and 288.

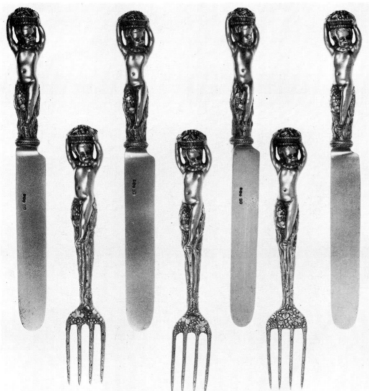

Figure 287. *'Bacchanal' dessert service. Silver-gilt examples from a set of twelve each of knives and forks. London 1820 (one fork 1816), Edward Farrell. Courtesy Phillips.*

Figure 288. *'Bacchanal' dessert spoons. Silver-gilt examples from a set of ten. London, 1816, Edward Farrell. Courtesy Phillips.*

Historicism

Other than the various nineteenth century patterns, such as Elizabethan and Venetian which, although not in themselves direct copies of more ancient forms, did incorporate earlier decorative detail, there were some direct or fairly direct copies based on much earlier English and Continental spoons.

The most famous of the early spoons to be copied regularly is the Anointing or Coronation Spoon from the English regalia. On various occasions, particularly coronations, from the latter part of the nineteenth century onwards, reproductions have been made, ranging from coffee to serving spoons. Historicist dessert services can also be found. However, the majority of pieces found will be for serving. Table services are unlikely.

Building a service other than dessert would not be possible, though even this would be very difficult, and it is best to regard such pieces as individual serving pieces.

See Figures 289-292.

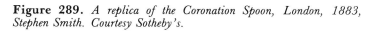

Figure 289. *A replica of the Coronation Spoon, London, 1883, Stephen Smith. Courtesy Sotheby's.*

Figure 290. *An early nineteenth century dessert serving spoon based on an early English seal top spoon. Formerly in the Royal Collection. Courtesy Sotheby's.*

Figure 291. *A Victorian dessert service based on Italian sixteenth century designs, London 1869/77, Henry Holland. Courtesy Phillips.*

Figure 292. *Nineteenth century rococo revival. Silver-gilt dessert spoons of mid-eighteenth century rococo form. Two from a set of twelve, London, (10) 1823/24, Charles Rawlings; (2) 1850, Francis Higgins. See also gold teaspoons, Figure 303. Courtesy Sotheby's.*

290

289

291

292

Onslow or Scroll

A pattern first produced in its recognised form about 1760 both with and without shoulders, and manufactured intermittently to the present day. Rudimentary forms can be found in the 1730s (particularly ladles) by Paul de Lamerie and others.

Onslow forks should normally have three prongs, but some late examples may be found with four.

The pattern is often said to have been named after Arthur Onslow (1691-1768) — 'The Great Speaker' of Parliament. There is, however, no evidence to support this idea, and in the Francis Higgins catalogue the pattern is named as Scroll.

In 1768 William and Thomas Chawner supplied a 'Scroll head Must d Spoon' to Parker & Wakelin (Garrard Mss., Victoria and Albert Museum), and it is probable that this refers to the Onslow pattern.

Genuine examples are difficult to find and most of these are serving pieces. Genuine services are of the utmost rarity; I know of only one straight service, and this is out of period being of Regency date. Building a service would be extremely difficult.

See Figures 293-296.

Pitfalls

Fakes are numerous, produced by cutting the end off an Old English or late Hanoverian piece and soldering on a cast Onslow end. Genuine Onslow should have a scarf join, whereas fakes often have butt joins.

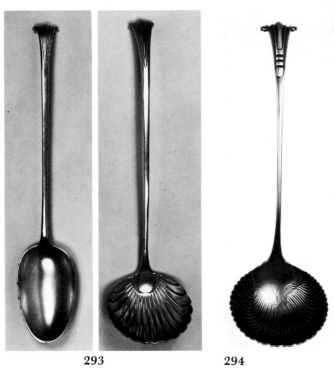

293 **294**

Figure 295. *Onslow pattern. Three eighteenth century table spoons originally Hanoverian or Old English patterns, legally converted in 1880 and 1882 by Charles Stuart Harris into Onslow pattern. The bowl decoration would have been carried out at the same time. Notice the additions marks at the top of the stem. Courtesy Phillips.*

Figure 296. *Detail of Figure 295 showing shoulder join, additions marks and original marks on legally converted Onslow pattern. Courtesy Phillips.*

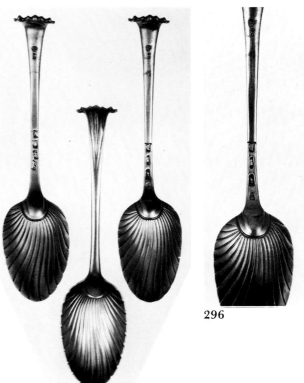

296

Figure 293. *Onslow pattern gravy spoon and soup ladle. Eighteenth century. Private collection.*

Figure 294. *Onslow pattern, an early form. Soup ladle, London, made between August 1753 and June 1754, the period of the partnership of William Turner and James Williams. Courtesy Phillips.*

295

Figure 297. *A selection of mid-eighteenth century pierced-handle condiment spoons and teaspoons. Courtesy Victoria and Albert Museum.*

Pierced-handle Flatware (see also Pierced Vine pp. 132-3, Rich Figure pp. 148-9, and Liberty pp. 155-6)

From the middle years of the eighteenth century pierced-handle tea and condiment spoons may be found occasionally. The designs are mostly baroque and rococo.

See Figure 297.

Pitfalls

Look for splits and repairs in the piercing.

Private Dies

It has always been and still is possible to commission flatware of an individual design, or with heraldic devices, etc., die-stamped instead of engraved on a stock pattern.

Most nineteenth century private die patterns were supplied through Hunt & Roskell (and their predecessors back to Paul Storr) to members of the peerage and other wealthy clients.

Hunt & Roskell would not themselves have produced these services, having them made first by Chawner & Co. and subsequently by Chawner's successor Francis Higgins.

Such pieces when found individually are fascinating but it is obviously impossible to build them into services.

See Figures 298 and 299.

Figure 299. *An unusual marrow scoop, die-stamped with crest and motto of the Marrowbone Club. Edinburgh, 1845, W. Cunningham. See also Figures 203 and 209 for die-stamped crests. Courtesy Phillips.*

Figure 298. *Private die variant of Pierced Vine pattern, incorporating heraldic devices and initials. Silver-gilt, London 1875/6, Hunt & Roskell overstamping Francis Higgins. Courtesy Sotheby's.*

Tea and Coffee Spoons (other than standard patterns)

Teaspoons have been included as part of the flatware service, and examples can be found of practically all the listed patterns.

There were, however, a number of designs which appear to have been produced only as sets of tea or coffee spoons. Many picture backs (see pp. 212-4) fit into this category as do the delightful mid-eighteenth century rococo examples which, often with a pair of sugar nippers, would be kept in a small shagreen covered case.

Boxes made to hold a pair of tea caddies and a sugar box would often be fitted with a section to hold a set of teaspoons, mote spoon and a pair of sugar nippers of quite individual designs.

In the late nineteenth century and through the twentieth century many cased sets of coffee spoons (usually six, sometimes twelve) have been produced, mostly bean end, apostle end or enamelled.

Enamelled examples usually have an engine-turned design over which a translucent enamel has been fired. Floral enamelled designs were also popular.

See Figures 300-305.

Figure 300. *Early eighteenth century silver-gilt teaspoons and a matching mote spoon, c.1705. Maker's mark only LA, a key above. Courtesy Sotheby's.*

Figure 301. *Early eighteenth century silver-gilt teaspoons (set of twelve) and a matching mote spoon, c.1720, unmarked. Courtesy Brand Inglis.*

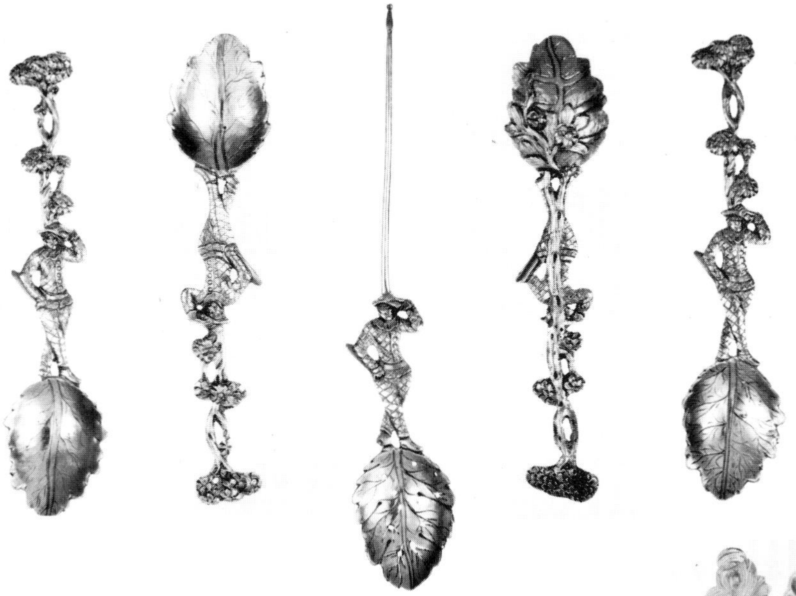

Figure 302. *Mid-eighteenth century silver-gilt harlequin teaspoons and mote spoon. Courtesy Sotheby's.*

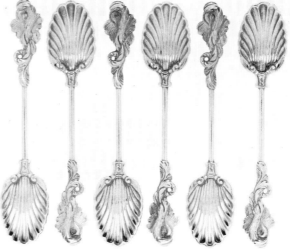

Figure 303. *Set of six 18ct. gold teaspoons in mid-eighteenth century rococo style. London, 1896, A. & A.H. Benson for Hunt & Roskell. Courtesy Sotheby's.*

Figure 304. *A mid-eighteenth century pair of tea caddies, sugar box and set of twelve teaspoons, a mote spoon and pair of sugar nippers all fitting into a contemporary black lacquered box with chinoiserie scenes. The teaspoons are formed as openwork vines, with ladybirds incorporated in the decoration. Maker's mark on teaspoons, mote spoon and sugar nippers script JD, acorn above. Courtesy Phillips.*

Figure 305. *Caddy box containing a pair of tea caddies and a sugar box (not shown), cream boat, set of twelve teaspoons, sugar nippers, mote spoon and pair of tea knives, London, 1735, Paul de Lamerie. The teaspoons are an interesting combination of rococo foliate scroll work and the extremely rare (for teaspoons) Whip pattern (see opposite). Courtesy Christie's.*

Whip (Whiplash)

The Whip pattern is one of the most rare of those known from the eighteenth century. Its name derives from the shape of the stem which is formed like a whip with its end bent over and coiled back round the stem. Until recently it was only known from mid-eighteenth century salt spoons. The discovery of the illustrated teaspoons, together with the examples by Paul de Lamerie which combine Whip with rococo naturalism, show that the range of this pattern must have been greater although no other examples have come to light.

In 1766 William and Thomas Chawner supplied Parker & Wakelin with 'Twisted handle salt spoons' (Garrard Mss., Workmen's Ledger No. 2, Victoria and Albert Museum). This may refer to the Whip pattern, although salt spoons with twisted handles of other patterns do occur at this period, such as the Onslow.

See Figures 306 and 307.

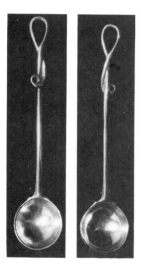

Figure 306. *A pair of mid-eighteenth century plain whip-handled salt spoons. Private collection.*

Figure 307. *Whip pattern. Set of six mid-eighteenth century teaspoons. These are the only known examples of teaspoons in the pure form of this pattern. Courtesy Victoria and Albert Museum.*

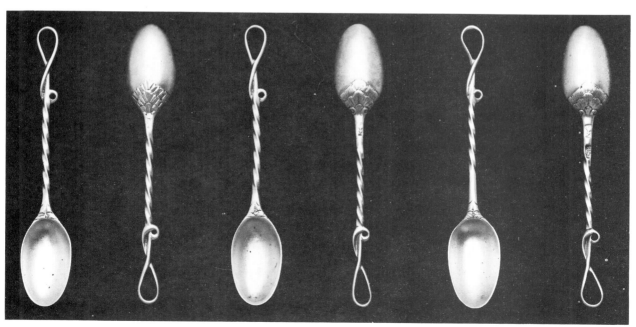

Figure 308. *Plain late eighteenth century Old English pattern serving tongs.*

Figure 309. *Nineteenth century Fiddle, Thread and Shell pattern serving tongs. Notice the broader blades.*

Figure 310. *Sprung serving tongs of the late eighteenth century (c.1775). Courtesy Phillips.*

Figure 311. *Scissor action serving tongs of the late eighteenth century (c.1775). Courtesy Phillips.*

Serving Pieces
(in alphabetical order)

Asparagus Forks

In 1770 William and Thomas Chawner supplied 'a 5 prong^d Asparagus Fork' to Parker & Wakelin (Garrard Mss., Victoria and Albert Museum).

It is possible that the flat bladed serving forks of the eighteenth century may have been for this purpose.

Not illustrated.

Asparagus Tongs (steak tongs, sandwich tongs)

Serving tongs for asparagus have been made since the mid-eighteenth century and may be divided into two principal groups — the u-shaped sprung tongs and those with a scissor action.

It is debatable whether some of these were intended for steak or asparagus, one view being that the narrow-bladed tongs were for steak and the broad-bladed for asparagus. There is also the question whether some, especially the broad-bladed examples of the nineteenth century, may have been intended for sandwiches. As the possibility of multi-function should also be considered, it is perhaps best to regard such pieces as being serving tongs. The late nineteenth century Higgins price book, however, lists only asparagus tongs.

Stylistically eighteenth century examples have similar designs to contemporary sugar tongs (see Sugar Tongs, pp. 198-200) of both the u-type and the spring action type. In the nineteenth century, however, the styles of contemporary flatware are followed more closely, since by this time they tended to be supplied with services rather than as individual pieces.

In 1772 Thomas Chawner supplied Parker & Wakelin with 'a pair of Asparagus Tongs Laureld 4oz. 5dwts.' (Garrard Mss., Victoria and Albert Museum).

See Figures 308-311.

Pitfalls

These are much the same as for sugar tongs, the most common being splits and repaired splits with the u-type. With the more rare spring action tongs it is, of course, important that the spring should be intact. As with sugar nippers of scissor type the two parts should fit firmly together. If they are loose, this can indicate either that they have had a hard life or been badly strained.

Basting and Gravy Spoons (see also Straining Spoons, p. 194)

The distinction between basting and gravy spoons tends to be one of size and date rather than of function.

Large serving spoons up to the end of the Hanoverian pattern (see Hanoverian pattern pp. 83-94) are usually described as basting spoons, while the smaller examples, starting with Old English pattern (see Old English pp. 94-107), are usually described as gravy spoons.

Large spoons exist and are mentioned in inventories and wills before the end of the seventeenth century, and up to the mid-eighteenth century their use would appear to have been confined to the kitchen. A good illustration of this is to be found with a Paul de Lamerie bill in the Mildmay Accounts:

> May 22nd 1733
> To a large kitchen spoon 3oz. 10dwts. at 6/- per oz. £1/1/0
> Fashion 7/6
> Engraving the crest and coronet 1/6

Examples of basting and gravy spoons will be found for all patterns of flatware with the possible exception of those patterns produced only in dessert services.

During the late seventeenth and early eighteenth centuries some particularly fine examples were made with hollow cannon handles (Figure 312) which are unusual amongst flatware in that they were made in several pieces. One particularly fine and rare example of this type has a marrow scoop which screws into the handle (Figure 314).

See Figures 312-314.

Pitfalls

Dents on early cannon handles are difficult to repair.

Figure 312. *Basting spoons of the cannon handle type and of the Dog Nose pattern. Private collection.*

Figure 313. *Old English pattern gravy spoon of the late eighteenth century. Private collection.*

Figure 314. *A very rare cannon handle basting spoon with marrow scoop screwing into the handle. 13 ¾ ins. long. London, 1751, John Barrett. The bowl and handle stamped with the name WOOD. Courtesy Phillips.*

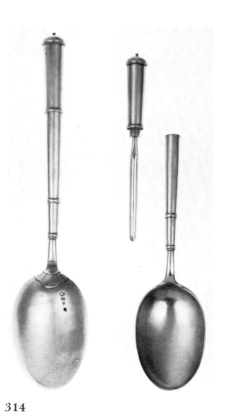

313

312

314

Butter Knives

The first examples are found in the very late eighteenth century when they replaced the butter spade. Early examples normally have an ivory handle, often stained green. By the late Regency most examples have a scimitar blade and 'spoon' handle in one of the usual patterns, butter knives now being made to go with flatware services (see Figure 202).

During the nineteenth and early twentieth centuries knife handles were produced using mother-of-pearl, agate and other materials. Earlier examples were normally at least dessert spoon size and could be as large as table spoon size, but by the late nineteenth century and through the twentieth century there has been a reduction in size to about that of a teaspoon.

Pitfalls

Odd 'spoon' handle fish knives could be mistaken for butter knives.

Splits at junction of blade and handle can be a problem. Some Birmingham examples were made with rather thin blades, look out for splits and repairs in these.

Butter Spades

Butter spades are quite rare, most examples dating from the middle and latter years of the eighteenth century, although earlier examples are known.

The usual form is that of a triangular or heart shaped blade with silver or turned wood or ivory handle. In the case of silver handles the design is normally Hanoverian. Few were made after the late eighteenth century when they were replaced by butter knives (see above).

See Figures 315 and 316.

Pitfalls

Conversions from contemporary spoons are the most serious, so it is best to obtain examples which are marked on the blade. Always be suspicious of any with bottom marked handles as these are usually the conversions.

315

316

Figure 315. *Late eighteenth century butter spade with green stained turned ivory handle. Courtesy M. McAleer.*

Figure 316. *An unusual ivory and silver butter spade, unmarked, c.1800. Courtesy Phillips.*

Figure 317. *Green stained ivory handled cheese scoop. London, 1822. Courtesy C.J. Vander.*

Figure 318. *A rare Trefid condiment spoon of the late seventeenth century. Private collection.*

Figure 319. *Old English pattern small pierced bowl condiment ladle of the late eighteenth century. Private collection.*

318   319

Cheese Scoops

Most eighteenth century and some nineteenth century examples have a strong stem with scoop end and an ivory handle, the most interesting of which incorporate a pusher to remove the cheese.

From the early nineteenth century examples were made completely of silver, matching the flatware patterns of the day.

See Figure 317; see also Figure 268.

Pitfalls

Splits and repaired splits in the stem should be looked for carefully. Once a scoop has a split it is no longer strong enough to be used properly. However, splits in the ivory of the handles are on the whole less serious, and the affect on the value of a piece will depend on how much the split detracts from the appearance of the handle.

Condiment Ladles and Spoons (see also Cream Ladles, Mustard Spoons, Salt Spoons, Sauce Ladles, Toddy Ladles)

Small ladles of various patterns, which do not fit happily into the more common categories, were made for such spices as cayenne, cinnamon and mustard. Spoons are sometimes found attached to the stoppers of condiment bottles (Figure 344) and some of the individual examples found today certainly started life in this way. Others were made for condiment vases; in 1767, for example, Isaac Callard supplied Parker & Wakelin with '3 vase spoons' (Garrard Mss., Victoria and Albert Museum).

See Figures 318 and 319.

Pitfalls

The spoons which have been separated from stoppers often appear to be cut off at the top; they are generally of a rather small size and usually from the Regency period.

Conversions from teaspoons also occur and the proportions of such examples are generally poor.

Examples exist which started life as sugar tongs and this should always be borne in mind when examining any unusually proportioned examples.

Cream Ladles

These small ladles, approximately between the size of condiment ladles and sauce ladles, were mostly made in the second half of the eighteenth century for the cream pails and piggins of the period and follow the contemporary flatware styles.

See Figure 320.

Pitfalls

Beware of conversions from other spoons, particularly of dessert size, and always look carefully for splits both in the stem and where the bowl joins the stem.

In Scotland both sauce and toddy ladles were made in similar sizes.

Dessert or Fruit Serving Pieces

Serving spoons of a highly decorative form for serving fruit have been produced in the nineteenth and twentieth centuries. These were mostly made to match dessert services. Earlier spoons were often decorated for this purpose and are mostly referred to as berry spoons.

See Figure 321; see also Figures 69, 70, 290, 291 and 298.

Figure 320. *Left, Fiddle Thread pattern small bowl ladle. London, 1863, Chawner & Co. This particular type could equally well be a condiment ladle; right, Fiddle pattern cream ladle. Exeter, 1818, SL. Courtesy M. McAleer.*

Figure 321. *A fruit or dessert serving set by Francis Higgins, London, 1883 (sifter) and 1887 (spoons). Courtesy Phillips.*

Figure 322. *Fiddle pattern fish slice with oblong blade. Dublin, 1819, J. Fray. Courtesy M. McAleer.*

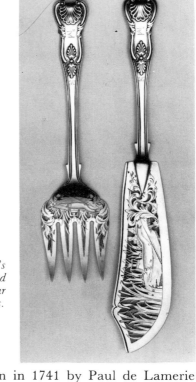

Figure 323. *King's pattern fish slice and fork, the slice of scimitar form. Courtesy Sotheby's.*

Fish Slices and Servers (see also Trowels)

The earliest known example was made in London in 1741 by Paul de Lamerie (Farrer Collection, Ashmolean Museum, Oxford). It is of trowel form, is made entirely of silver and has its oval blade pierced and engraved with dolphins and fish within rococo scrollwork.

There is quite a gap before the next examples are found, in the last quarter of the eighteenth century. These have a symmetrical boat-shaped blade and either an ivory or loaded silver handle (Figure 54).

At the turn of the century the blades are normally oblong or canted oblong (Figure 322) and the handles still made of either ivory or loaded silver. This type is particularly useful since it can more easily be used for serving other things as well as fish.

In the early nineteenth century slices changed quite radically; the blade and handle began to be made in one piece (as indeed was the earliest example) and the handles began to follow the flatware patterns of the day, while the blade became asymmetric taking on the appearance of a stunted scimitar. This form, sometimes with ivory or loaded silver handles, has continued through to the present day. Forks quite often accompany these slices (Figure 323).

Fish slices are pierced in two ways, either with fish of various types or with geometric forms.

Pitfalls

Always hold fish slices up to the light to see if there are any splits in the piercing, then examine the piercing for any repairs.

With ivory and loaded silver handles inspect for splits and, in the case of the latter, repaired splits. Make sure also that the handle is contemporary, later replacements generally being out of proportion. The maker's mark on a loaded silver handle will normally differ from that on the blade since haft or handle making was a specialised branch of silversmithing (see Knives, p. 46).

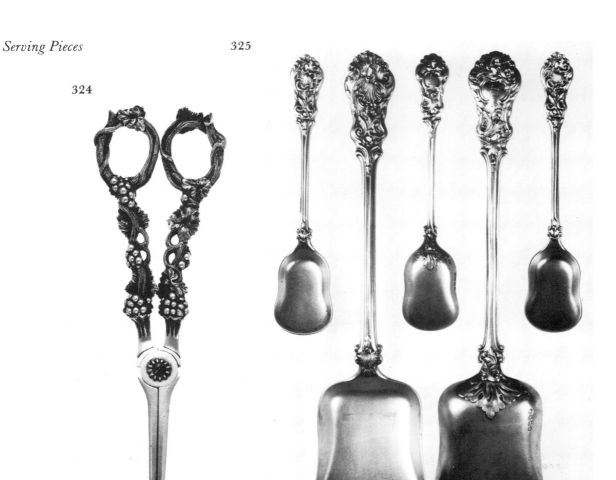

324   325

Figure 324. *Grape shears. Silver-gilt, London, 1842, Charles Rawlings & William Summers. Courtesy Sotheby's.*

Figure 325. *A pair of ice or ice cream spades with part of a set of six ice cream spoons. London, 1866/77, Geo. W. Adams of Chawner & Co., overstruck by Robert Garrard. Courtesy Sotheby's.*

Grape Shears

Although known from the late eighteenth century the majority date from the nineteenth century. Some of the finest were made during the Regency and these are frequently gilded and decorated with grapes and vines. With some grape shears steel cutting edges are let into the silver, since silver has a bad cutting edge. The most popular of the designs was the grape and vine, but all patterns of the nineteenth century may be found.

Grape shears were made as separate items as well as to go with flatware services. See Figure 324.

Pitfalls

Strained or worn joints are common and shears with these will not cut properly, though it may be possible for a silversmith to improve them.

Splits and repaired splits in the arms should always be carefully looked for. Quite a force has to be applied to the arms in order to cut the grape stems and once a weakness has developed it will probably get worse.

Ice Spades and Spoons

Found mostly from the Regency and later nineteenth century these serving pieces are easily distinguished by their oblong spade-shaped bowls. Examples can be as large as a gravy spoon. Most were made to go with flatware services and are found in the patterns of the nineteenth century.

In 1772 Wood & Filkin supplied Parker and Wakelin with a 'threaded ice spoon' (Garrard Mss., Victoria and Albert Museum).

Since they have quite a tough job to perform, most examples are made very solidly and are of a good weight.

See Figure 325.

Jam Spoons

Jam spoons have been produced from the middle years of the nineteenth century. They have a flat spade-like bowl which is often engraved; in addition some have a small hook for hanging the spoon on the side of the pot.

Most were made as individual pieces, often with mother-of-pearl, ivory or, more rarely, agate handles. Examples will also be found of standard patterns made to go with services.

Pitfalls

An ice spoon found on its own could be mistaken for a jam spoon; however, the latter, although it has a flat bowl, also has sides to the bowl (see above).

Marrow Scoops (see also Marrow Spoons)

Scoops to remove the marrow jelly from bones evolved from the earlier marrow spoon during the reign of Queen Anne. The characteristic form is that of two different size scoops joined in the centre by a short stem; the whole scoop should be made from one piece of silver. Marks will be struck on the central stem, while crests, initials, etc. will usually be engraved on the underside of the larger of the two scoops.

A scoop will normally have both bowls open side up when placed on the table, although during the first half of the eighteenth century it would have been placed open bowl down in the French manner. Rare examples can be found which have the bowls facing in opposite directions.

The development of the marrow scoop through the eighteenth century is essentially that of changing proportions; the overall length gradually increased through the century, and the three sections (two scoops and stem) became more distinct with stronger angles and curves.

In the late eighteenth century and through the nineteenth, marrow scoops were produced in the various flatware patterns, the pattern being found on the central stem.

The end of the marrow scoop came with meat rationing in the Second World War when it was not possible to buy joints of the size which would contain a bone from which marrow could be scooped. Today the scoops are frequently used as honey scoops.

See Figures 299 and 326.

Pitfalls

Fakes are made by reshaping eighteenth century table spoons, though the proportions of these are not generally very good, the scoops tending also to be rather thin.

Splits and repaired splits in the stem are a danger. There should be no solder join anywhere on a scoop since they were always made from one piece of silver.

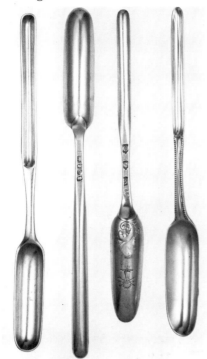

Figure 326. *Marrow scoops. From left to right: plain, London, 1757, Richard Gosling; plain, London, 1803, Peter, Ann & William Bateman; fancy back, London, 1749, Ebenezer Coker; beaded, London, 1774, Hester Bateman. Courtesy Phillips.*

Figure 327. *Marrow spoons all in very good condition. From left to right: gilded marrow spoon of about 1695. Notice the engraved stylised leaf work and the short length of the stem; George I marrow basting spoon, London 1724. Notice the proportionately longer stem; a very rare example because of its size; mid-eighteenth century marrow spoon of table size. This is the most common size and form. Notice that the crest is engraved on the front of the stem; a typical eighteenth century marrow scoop for comparison. Private collection.*

326

327

Marrow Spoons (see also Marrow Scoops)

The marrow spoon is basically a spoon the handle of which is formed as a scoop for the removal of marrow from beef bones.

Examples can be found as early as the 1690s and these examples are contemporary with Trefid spoons. Most seventeenth century examples are gilded and engraved with stylised leaf work on the stem and on either side of the rat tail on the back of the bowl. The same form of decoration is found on contemporary Trefid spoons and forks.

It is an interesting point that, from their introduction, marrow spoons are found as an integral part of many travelling canteens.

A good many eighteenth century examples can be found, although towards the end of the century they become scarcer. Throughout the century plain examples occur most frequently.

Few examples are found from the nineteenth or twentieth centuries. Marrow scoops were far more popular by this time and it would appear that these developed directly from marrow spoons in the early years of the eighteenth century.

Size varies from tea to basting spoon, though the majority of examples are of table spoon size. An example is known with a mote spoon bowl; a marrow fork is also known which has been dated to about 1670, as is a cannon handled basting spoon with marrow scoop incorporated into the handle (see Figure 314).

Marking is fairly straightforward: early specimens (1690s) are normally only partially marked, while examples from the eighteenth and nineteenth centuries are mostly fully marked. In both cases the marks will be found on the back of the stem.

The stem gradually increases in length during the eighteenth century, the increase being particularly marked in the early years. The short length of seventeenth century marrow spoon stems is probably a contributory factor in their being only partially marked.

See Figure 327.

Pitfalls

Look out for the usual signs of poor condition: worn bowls, splits, repairs and reshaped bowls.

The most important individual pitfall with this group is the conversion of ordinary spoons. This is done either by reshaping the original spoon handle to form a scoop, or by removing the top of the handle of a spoon and substituting a completely new scoop end.

With engraved and gilded examples make sure that both the engraving and the gilding are original.

Mustard Spoons

These are mostly found from the second half of the eighteenth century and on through to the present day, and occur in practically all patterns. During the nineteenth century a number of quite individual novelty forms were produced. Late nineteenth and twentieth century examples are usually of a small size.

The elongated bowl is the characteristic of the mustard spoon, but it must be remembered that this same bowl shape is found with some egg spoons. Such egg spoons are normally rather larger than mustard spoons and are frequently found in sets of six or more, while mustard spoons are mostly found in pairs.

There is evidence that Trefid condiment spoons (Figure 318) were used for mustard. See Figure 328.

Pitfalls

Apart from the possibility of confusion with some egg spoons, these should present no real problems, while their low value has saved them from the attentions of the fakers. Some teaspoons have had bowls reshaped to make mustard spoons.

Figure 328. *Mustard spoons. Notice the much smaller size of the twentieth century Lily pattern example on the right. Courtesy M. McAleer.*

Figure 329. *A pickle fork in Princess No. 1 pattern, from an extensive service by Geo. W. Adams of Chawner & Co. Courtesy Phillips.*

328

329

Pickle Forks and Spoons

These relatively modern additions to the range of serving pieces were first produced in the middle to late years of the nineteenth century. They are either of a standard pattern made as part of a service, or of individual design, usually with knife handles made of a variety of materials such as mother-of-pearl, ivory or agate.

Pickle spoons range in length from about that of a dessert spoon up to that of a table spoon.

The forks are two or three prong with barbs on the outer prongs. The bowl of the spoon is about the same size as a teaspoon.

See Figure 329.

Pitfalls

Iced-tea spoons, made for the American market over a similar period of time, could be mistaken for pickle spoons if found individually.

Punch Ladles

Most examples date from the eighteenth and early nineteenth century. Early eighteenth century examples have an oval or round bowl and a turned wood handle, but by the mid-eighteenth century shaped oval double-lipped examples are found, again with turned wood handles.

Much lighter ladles were made in the second half of the eighteenth century, usually of twisted whalebone although occasionally an example with a silver handle may be found. A rare mid-eighteenth century variety has a shell bowl.

The bowls of the later ladles may be divided into two groups: those with hallmarked bowls which are mostly oval and often have a lip; those made from silver coins, of crown size, and as a result not hallmarked. These are usually round and have the edge of the coin left intact around the top edge of the bowl, with a silver coin, usually a sixpence or a shilling, set into the base.

William Lestourgeon supplied Parker & Wakelin with dollar ladles and crown ladles in 1766 (Garrard Mss., Victoria and Albert Museum).

In Scotland some quite small examples, known as toddy ladles, were produced and these are often found in sets (see p.201).

See Figures 330 and 331.

Pitfalls

Punch ladles are particularly prone to splits and repairs on the stem which joins bowl to handle.

Figure 330. *Early eighteenth century punch ladle with simple plain bowl and turned wooden handle. Courtesy Phillips.*

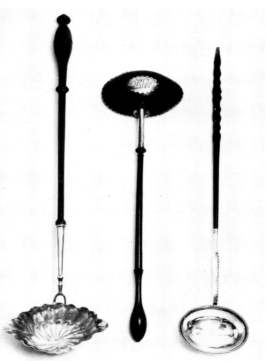

Figure 331. *Punch ladles. Left to right: mid-eighteenth century double lipped with turned wood handle; unusual mid-eighteenth century with silver mounted coconut bowl and turned wood handle; late eighteenth century with twisted whalebone handle. Courtesy Phillips.*

Salad Servers (see also Asparagus Forks)

Dating mostly from the second half of the eighteenth century and onwards, salad servers comprise a spoon of gravy spoon size, and a fork of the same size and shape. The forks are often shaped in a similar way to the spoon bowl and usually have five or more prongs.

In 1772 Thomas Chawner supplied two '6 pronged Salad Forks 10oz. 11dwts.' to Parker & Wakelin (Garrard Mss., Victoria and Albert Museum).

See Figures 332 and 333.

Pitfalls

Care must be taken to examine the forks carefully to make sure that they are not conversions from spoons. These are generally quite obvious.

Figure 332. *Old English pattern salad servers. Nineteenth century. Courtesy Phillips.*

Figure 333. *Old English pattern salad fork. George III, by George Smith and William Fearn. Private Collection.*

Salt Spoons and Shovels

Although magnificent vessels had been made to contain salt throughout the medieval, Tudor and Caroline periods, it was not until the end of the seventeenth century that any form of spoon or shovel appears to have been made for use with salt.

We learn from *The Boke of Kervyng* that salt was to be taken with a clean knife. The *Babees Book* of 1475 also pointed out that 'The salte also touche not in his salere with nokyns mete'.

The earliest form to be found is the shovel. Most of these are of Hanoverian pattern and were produced up to about the 1770s. Contemporary with these are examples which have shell bowls. Whip handled salt spoons are occasionally found from the middle years of the eighteenth century (see Whip pattern, p. 177).

With the introduction of the Old English pattern, the salt spoon took on its modern form with a deep round or oval bowl with gilt interior. From this period on all the usual flatware patterns are to be found. Late eighteenth to mid-nineteenth century examples tend to be of a very good size. Many novelty forms were produced together with examples of revived rococo, Gothic, etc. decoration during the Victorian and Edwardian periods.

From the late nineteenth century on salt spoons are of a much smaller size.

See Figure 334.

Pitfalls

Be very careful as regards condition since salt corrodes silver very rapidly, and a spoon which has hardly been used can, if it has been stored in the wrong conditions, be badly corroded.

Figure 334. *Salt shovels and spoons. Notice first the three different sizes: left (3), mid-eighteenth century medium size; centre (2), early nineteenth century large size; right (2), twentieth century small size.*

Left to right, Old English pattern, c.1770, transitional form between shovel and spoon; Hanoverian shovel, c.1760; Onslow pattern with shell bowl, c.1760; Old English Bead pattern, nineteenth century; Fiddle Thread pattern, nineteenth century; Onslow, early twentieth century; Hanoverian early twentieth century. Courtesy M. McAleer/Private Collection.

Sauce Ladles

Examples dating from before the middle years of the eighteenth century are rare, and some of the most magnificent are the rococo examples of this period by such makers as Lamerie, Cripps and Kandler.

From the second half of the eighteenth century through to the present day sauce ladles have been produced to go with all the flatware patterns.

Three principal bowl shapes are found: oval, round and shell. The vast majority of sauce ladles have bowls with a curved base, though some nineteenth century examples may be found with flat bases similar to those found on sugar sifter spoons.

Scottish examples of a smaller size than English sauce ladles, and often found in sets, are known as toddy ladles (see p. 201). Irish examples are known with lips (see Figure 51).

See Figures 335 and 336.

Pitfalls

Always examine very carefully for splits and repaired splits, particularly with shell bowl examples which are vulnerable to splits along the lines of the fluting.

Figure 335. *Onslow pattern sauce ladle with shell bowl. London, c.1760, Paul Callard. Courtesy Phillips.*

Figure 336. *Left to right, round bowl, Lamerie pattern; round bowl, flat base, Vine pattern; oval bowl, Victoria pattern; oval bowl, flat base, Elizabethan pattern. Courtesy Sotheby's.*

Skewers

The majority of skewers date from the second half of the eighteenth and first half of the nineteenth century.

There are two basic divisions of size and two of style. As regards size the larger examples were for meat and the smaller ones for poultry and references are therefore made to meat skewers or poultry skewers.

The two basic styles are those with blades of oblong-shaped cross section of the eighteenth century, and those of lozenge-shaped cross section of the late eighteenth and on through the nineteenth century.

More detailed variation in style can be found at the ends and with the rings. There may be shell mounts, foliate scroll mounts, reeded or beaded decoration. During the nineteenth century examples were produced to match current flatware patterns.

See Figures 337 and 338.

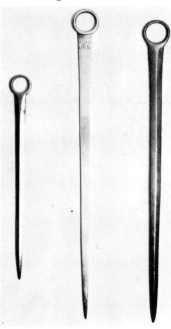

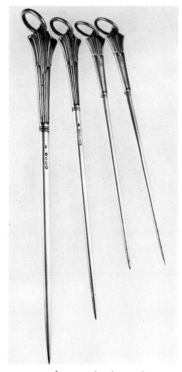

Figure 337. *Late eighteenth century skewers. Left to right, poultry, lozenge cross section; meat, oblong cross section; meat, lozenge cross section. Courtesy Phillips.*

Figure 338. *Albany pattern meat and poultry skewers, 14¼ ins., 12¼ ins. and 10ins. long. London, 1883, Elkington & Co. overstriking another. Courtesy Sotheby's.*

Soup Ladles

Although found from the first half of the eighteenth century the majority of soup ladles date from after this, and since they were usually produced to go with flatware services examples of most of the known patterns may be found. Some very fine rococo ladles were made in the mid-eighteenth century, the handles of which often terminated in an eagle's head. A good many mid-eighteenth century examples are found with maker's marks only (Figures 340 and 341).

Three types of bowl are found: round, oval and shell.

During the late nineteenth century a ladle of revolutionary design was produced by Hukin & Heath (see Dr. Christopher Dresser, Figure 249 and p. 155).

See Figures 339-343.

Pitfalls

Soup ladles are particularly prone to splits in the lower half of the stem and the bowl on either side of the junction with the stem.

With shell bowl ladles always look for splits or repaired splits in the fluting.

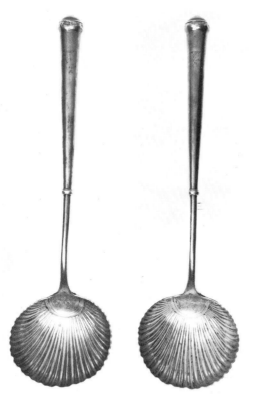

Figure 339. *A rare and unusual pair of mid-eighteenth century soup ladles with cannon handles and shell bowls. Unmarked. Courtesy Phillips.*

Figure 340. *A pair of mid-eighteenth century rococo soup ladles. London, c.1745, Peter Archambo. Maker's mark only struck three times (see p. 41). Courtesy Sotheby's.*

339

340

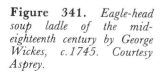

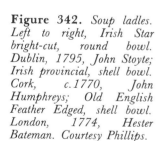

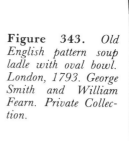

Figure 341. *Eagle-head soup ladle of the mid-eighteenth century by George Wickes, c.1745. Courtesy Asprey.*

Figure 343. *Old English pattern soup ladle with oval bowl. London, 1793. George Smith and William Fearn. Private Collection.*

Figure 342. *Soup ladles. Left to right, Irish Star bright-cut, round bowl. Dublin, 1795, John Stoyte; Irish provincial, shell bowl. Cork, c.1770, John Humphreys; Old English Feather Edged, shell bowl. London, 1774, Hester Bateman. Courtesy Phillips.*

Spice Spoons (see also Condiment Ladles)

Small spoons intended for spice are sometimes found from the eighteenth century. In 1767 Isaac Callard supplied Parker & Wakelin with pepper spoons. A year later, William and Thomas Chawner supplied Parker & Wakelin with a 'Small Kyan Spoon'; the same account also gives mention of 'Drilling a pepper spoon' (Garrard Mss., Victoria and Albert Museum).

Quite tiny spoons are sometimes found attached to the stoppers of spice bottles in cruet sets. An amusing example is sometimes found with the head of the devil, indicating cayenne pepper.

See Figure 344.

Straining Spoons

The function of the straining spoon was for the serving of vegetables, etc. where juices had to be separated from solids.

Most examples of these scarce spoons date from the eighteenth and early nineteenth century, a good proportion being found from Ireland.

Essentially they are gravy or basting spoons which incorporate some form of straining device. Indeed some examples have detachable strainers, which not only make cleaning easier but also mean that the spoon may perform two functions, as either a gravy or a straining spoon.

Examples were usually made to go with services and are of the various flatware patterns of the eighteenth and nineteenth centuries.

The strainer itself was formed in various ways, the most simple by partially piercing the bowl itself. Alternatively half the bowl could be covered with a pierced plate. However, the most common straining spoons have a central pierced divider in the bowl. Both the covered bowl and the central divider type may be detachable.

See Figures 345 and 346; also Church Strainer Spoons, pp.204-5.

Pitfalls

Ordinary gravy spoons with recently added strainers can occur, and in such cases the silver of the strainer will usually be of a different colour to that of the spoon.

Sugar Nippers

Sugar nippers were made predominantly during two periods: the mid-eighteenth century, often to go with sets of teaspoons, and the mid-nineteenth century. To a lesser extent they have also been produced through to the present day.

The earliest may be dated to about 1715 when they replaced the andiron type of sugar tong.

There are various useful guides to date based on variations of bowls, arms, finger grips and position of marks.

The earliest nippers, c.1715 to the early 1730s, have rat tails on the bowls. (Some rare early examples with a 'box' hinge are found with shell bowls.) With the disappearance of the rat tail in the 1730s a plain bowl is found, quickly followed in the latter 1730s by the shell bowl, which then continues for the remainder of the eighteenth century.

As to arms, those up to the 1730s are straight, usually with baluster mouldings. Scrolling arms are found in the mid-eighteenth century, while the 1770s saw a return to straight arms, often tapering and terminating in a small scroll.

Finger grips are usually simple rings with early nippers but may be variously shaped with later examples.

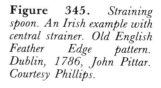

Figure 345. *Straining spoon. An Irish example with central strainer. Old English Feather Edge pattern. Dublin, 1786, John Pittar. Courtesy Phillips.*

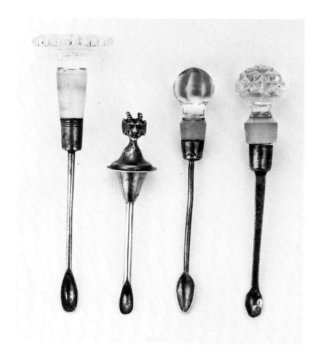

Figure 344. *Bottle stoppers with spoons attached, from early nineteenth century condiment bottles. The example with the devil's head indicates the stopper comes from a cayenne pepper bottle. Courtesy M. McAleer.*

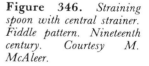

Figure 346. *Straining spoon with central strainer. Fiddle pattern. Nineteenth century. Courtesy M. McAleer.*

Nippers were mostly partially marked, usually with the maker's mark and standard mark only. Early nippers, up to about 1740, are marked in the bowls while later examples are marked on the finger grips. Some late examples may be found fully marked.

Two other important eighteenth century types may be found: rococo nippers of various forms (often unmarked) and the rare stork nippers, which are no longer accepted as sugar nippers.

Stork nippers have a claw fitted to one of their finger grips so that they may stand up. When opened (they are hinged at the top of their body) a baby, either fixed or loose, may be found inside. The beak of the stork is not very practical for gripping sugar and this type of nipper is now regarded as having been a ribbon puller.

By the 1770s sugar nippers were being rapidly replaced by sugar tongs. However, in the nineteenth century copies were produced of all the preceding century's forms. In addition some new novelty tongs were introduced such as wooden dolls, wishbones, monkeys and harlequins.

A useful guide to quality is to examine the hinges. These were made in one of two ways. Either the two halves were simply pinned together, or one half was put through the centre of two plates in the other (see Figure 347). Of the two forms the latter is the best.

See Figures 348-352.

Pitfalls

It is very difficult to find a pair of nippers which has not been repaired at some time in its life. Examine carefully for solder joins and assess each pair of nippers on the number of repairs and the competence with which they have been carried out.

During the nineteenth century a number of unmarked copies of rococo and stork nippers were produced. These are not normally as well finished as the eighteenth century originals.

Figure 347. *Detail to show the best form of hinge for sugar nippers. Courtesy Phillips.*

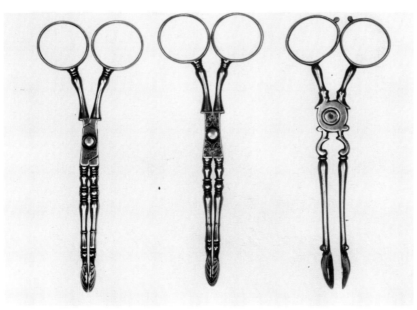

348

Figure 348. *Early sugar nippers. Left to right, straight baluster arms, shell grips, plain ring finger grips, c.1730, Henry Renaud; similar but silver-gilt and with an engraved 'box' hinge. Unmarked, c.1725; straight arms, rat tail bowls, c.1730, Richard Pargeter. Courtesy Phillips.*

Figure 349. *Mid-eighteenth century sugar nippers. Left to right, with scroll work arms, shell grips, c.1750; tapering straight arms, shell grips, c.1760; scroll work arms, shell grips. The early bright-cut engraving indicates a date in the 1760s or early 1770s. Courtesy Phillips.*

Figure 350. *Mid-eighteenth century rococo sugar nippers, both c.1750. Left, possibly by Philip Roker; right, unmarked. Courtesy Phillips.*

Figure 351. *Nineteenth century sugar nippers. Left to right, cast vine, London, 1827, William Eley; cast with butterfly hinge, Birmingham, 1840, Joseph Willmore; cast harlequin, Birmingham, 1839, Joseph Willmore. Courtesy Phillips.*

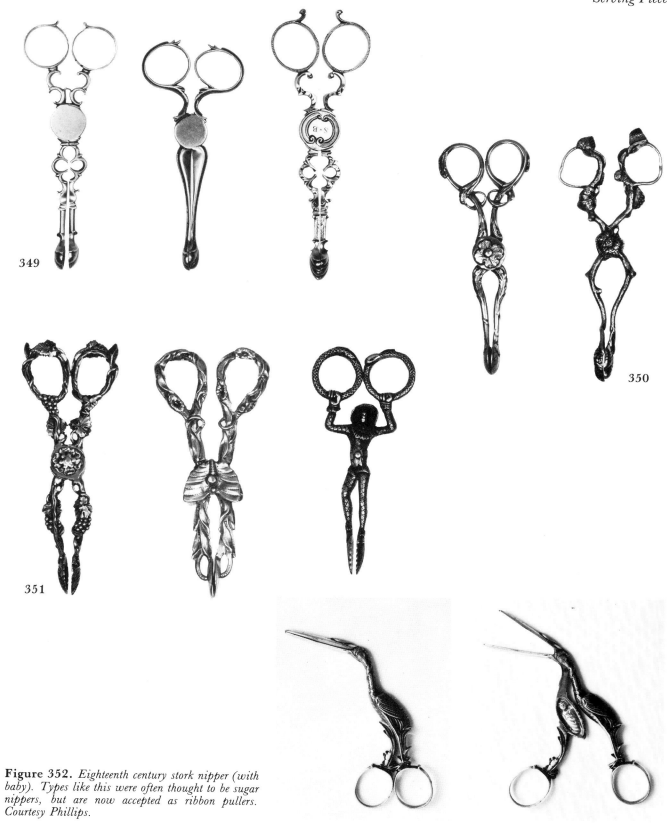

349

350

351

Figure 352. *Eighteenth century stork nipper (with baby). Types like this were often thought to be sugar nippers, but are now accepted as ribbon pullers. Courtesy Phillips.*

Sugar Sifter Spoons

Sugar sifter spoons have been produced from the mid-eighteenth century through to the present day. Since they were normally made as part of a service they naturally follow the flatware styles of the various periods. They are of the same size as sauce ladles.

See Figures 353 and 354.

Pitfalls

Sauce ladles which have been later pierced to resemble sugar sifter spoons are probably the greatest danger. Sifter spoons normally have flat bases to the bowls whereas sauce ladles have curved bases. See Figure 70 for a sauce ladle converted to a sugar sifter spoon.

Figure 353. *Sugar sifter spoons. Left, Fiddle Thread, early nineteenth century; right, Old English, c.1785. Courtesy Phillips.*

Figure 354. *Victorian sugar sifter spoon. Birmingham, 1854, Hilliard & Thomason. Courtesy Phillips.*

Sugar Spoons

Moist sugar or demerara spoons can be found from the early nineteenth century on. They were made to go with services and therefore are found in standard flatware patterns. Their shallow oblong bowls easily distinguish them from all but ice spoons and caddy spoons.

Not illustrated.

Pitfalls

Confusion with ice spoons (see Ice Cream Spoons page 206).

Confusion with caddy spoons: sugar spoons are normally larger and stouter. Few caddy spoons have oblong bowls.

Sugar Tongs (tea tongs)

Sugar or tea tongs (as they were referred to in the eighteenth century) were produced during two quite distinct periods.

The first was in the late seventeenth and early eighteenth century (up to about 1720) and tongs of this period are of the andiron or fire tong type. The bowls have rat tails and the stems or arms are quite slender. The 'curved' end, which was often shaped, usually has a baluster finial; some examples also have a screw-in spike running parallel to the arms which starts beneath this finial and could be used for unblocking spouts, as with mote spoons.

During the 1720s tongs were replaced by nippers (see pp. 194-7) and it was not until the 1770s that tongs were again made.

Examples from the 1770s are usually made in three pieces, these being the two cast, usually openwork, arms, and the sprung end section. Such examples are partially marked, usually maker's mark and standard mark, stamped approximately on the two solder joins. An unusual variant has the arms set at right angles to the sprung end section (see Figure 358).

By the 1780s tongs were mostly made from one piece of metal and the marks on such were first struck in the bowls. By the end of the eighteenth and on into the nineteenth century, tongs were more fully marked on the inside of the arms or on the inside of the curved end.

Sugar tongs were produced in practically all the known flatware patterns during the nineteenth century, although by the end of the nineteenth century their production was in decline. During this period and on into the twentieth century much smaller sugar tongs started to be made.

See Figures 356-360.

Pitfalls

All sugar tongs are especially susceptible to splits in their curved ends so always examine these carefully for repairs.

Most cast openwork tongs of the 1770s have been split and repaired at some stage, indeed it is very difficult to find any example of this type which has not been repaired, so look for added silver on the inside of the arms (see Figure 355).

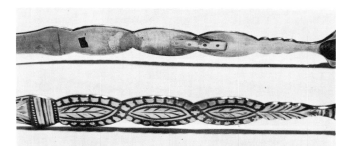

Figure 355. *Detail of cast arm sugar tongs. The solder join on the left is the join between the cast arm and the sprung end. The plate and solder join on the right is a bad, later repair. Courtesy Phillips.*

Figure 356. *Early sugar tongs. Left to right, c.1700 with hinged top and very small flat grips (it is suggested that this form may have served some other function, perhaps as a ribbon puller); c.1720 with shaped angular top; c.1720 with pierced rat tail bowls. This pair originally had a central screw-in spike. Courtesy Phillips.*

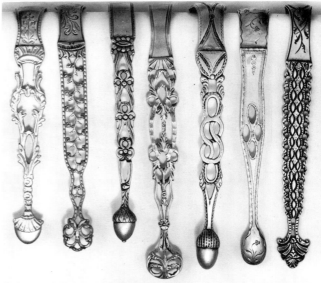

Figure 357. *A group of cast arm sugar tongs, c.1775, showing the tremendous variety of styles to be found. Courtesy Phillips.*

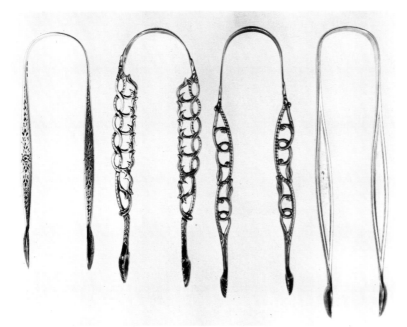

Figure 358. *Sugar tongs with arms at right angles to the sprung end section. Left and right, c.1790. Centre two with cast arms, c.1775. Courtesy Phillips.*

Figure 359. *Cast arm sugar tongs, c.1775. Courtesy Phillips.*

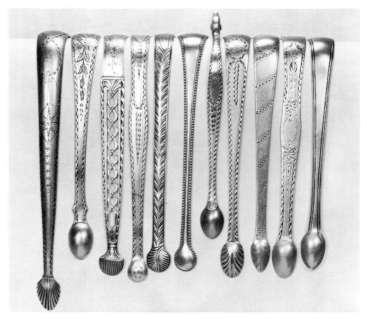

Figure 360. *Sugar tongs made from one piece of silver (except third from left which has cast arms, and seventh from left which has a central spring). Patterns include Irish Star Bright-cut, Old English Bead and Old English Thread. Courtesy Phillips.*

Toddy Ladles

Small ladles, mostly of the Old English and Fiddle patterns, were made in Scotland, principally during the early and middle years of the nineteenth century (Figure 361). Examples with twisted whalebone handles and looking like miniature punch ladles will also be found.

Ladles of this size when made in England or Ireland are normally referred to as cream ladles (see p. 182).

Figure 361. *Toddy ladles. The four outer ladles a set of four, Fiddle pattern. Aberdeen, c.1800, James Erskine; centre, one of a pair, Fiddle pattern. Dundee, c.1815, maker's mark WL. Courtesy Phillips.*

Trowels (fish or pudding; see also Fish Slices)

Serving trowels date mostly from the middle years of the eighteenth century. In 1745 Wakelin supplied the Earl of Kildare with a 'Pudding Trowle' (Garrard Mss., Victoria and Albert Museum). Trowels have a pierced triangular blade and turned wood handle. Marks are usually struck on the underside of the blade near to the handle, though as the piercing was carried out after hallmarking, marks have often been completely or partially lost.

William Plummer who specialised in pierced work was the most prolific maker of such trowels.

See Figure 362.

Pitfalls

As with all pierced work, splits and repaired splits are the greatest problem.

Do not confuse serving trowels with nineteenth century ceremonial trowels which have solid blades.

Figure 362. *Mid-eighteenth century serving trowel. Courtesy Phillips.*

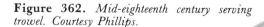

Miscellaneous Pieces

(in alphabetical order)

Caddy Spoons

The caddy spoon presents one of the most extensive collecting areas. The earliest are found in the 1760s (though the earliest known fully marked is 1777), and for about the next one hundred years large quantities were produced in seemingly infinite combinations of shape and decoration.

One can divide these spoons into two major groups: first those which follow the styles of contemporary flatware patterns (e.g. Old English, Fiddle, King's), and second those made using quite individual styles (e.g. jockey caps, eagles' wings and fish).

Those in the first group are the most common but still provide a wealth of variation for the collector, e.g. round bowls, oval bowls, shell bowls, pierced edge bowls, bowls with inset filigree panels, and plain and engraved bowls. With the various combinations the number of possible types is seemingly endless.

A good many will be found from the provinces, particularly Birmingham, and examples from York and Chester are known but rare. With the exception of

363

Figure 363. *Caddy spoons. The examples in the top row (two paston, one shovel) have hollow handles, typical of Birmingham, which are difficult to repair if dented. These and the other examples give an idea of the infinite variety to be found. Courtesy Phillips.*

364

Figure 364. *A selection of caddy spoons. The broom is a great rarity as is the plain fish and the two right hands; left hands are also extremely rare. The spoon above the broom has a natural shell as its bowl. The other examples show the variety to be found with the more ordinary caddy spoons. Courtesy M. McAleer.*

Birmingham caddy spoons, most provincial examples are in the more ordinary patterns such as Old English or Fiddle.

Scottish and Irish examples may be found, the latter often of a large size.

See Figures 363 and 364.

Pitfalls

All caddy spoons must be carefully examined for splits and repairs.

Fakes of rare types must be looked out for. Watch cases, for example, have been converted into jockey cap caddy spoons.

Conversions from teaspoons are frequently found, even of the more ordinary type. Look for solder joins between handle (or stem) and bowl where they should not be. Always be very wary of any gilded example.

See also Sugar Sifter Spoons, p. 198.

Christening Sets

Sets of individual dessert or slightly smaller size knives, forks and spoons have been produced as christening presents from at least the beginning of the nineteenth century. These were usually cased, often with a dish, bowl, beaker or mug and, from the late nineteenth century onwards, with a napkin ring.

Quite individual designs were often produced, one of the most appropriate (Figure 368) being based on Kate Greenaway characters.

See Figures 365-368.

365   366

Figure 365. *A George IV christening set. London, 1821, Charles Rawlings. Courtesy Sotheby's.*

Figure 366. *A magnificent early Victorian royal christening set. London, 1838, Paul Storr (spoon) and Theobalds & Atkinson. Courtesy Phillips.*

367 368

Figure 367. *A Victorian christening set. London, 1862/3, Francis Higgins. Courtesy Phillips.*

Figure 368. *A delightful Victorian parcel-gilt christening set, based on Kate Greenaway characters from her book* Under the Window, *1879. London, 1882, Sampson Mordan. Courtesy Phillips.*

Church Strainer Spoons

Spoons of various patterns have been used in church both before and during the period of production of flatware. Usually of table size, these spoons have their bowls pierced in order to remove foreign bodies from the wine to be used in Holy Communion.

See Figure 369.

Egg Spoons

Examples of egg spoons may be found from the late eighteenth century through to the present day. They were made to go either with flatware services or with egg cruets and most follow the contemporary flatware patterns.

Two bowl shapes are found, the oblong and the shield, the latter being the most distinct.

Oblong-bowled egg spoons can cause confusion because they so closely resemble mustard spoons of the nineteenth century. They are, however, normally a little larger than mustard spoons (very small mustard spoons are comparatively modern), and are found in sets.

In 1735 George Wickes sold to Mr. Desborrough 'A Eggspoon 2oz. 5dwts.'

(Garrard Mss., Victoria and Albert Museum). From the given weight and the fact that it was an individual spoon it is probable that this was a serving piece.

See Figure 370.

Pitfalls
Confusion with mustard spoons.

Figure 369. *A George II church strainer spoon. Dublin, 1736, Joseph Teafe. Courtesy M. McAleer.*

Figure 370. *Egg spoons. On the left an oblong bowl, Old English pattern. York, 1818, Barber & Whitwell; right, set of three shield or spade shaped bowls, Fiddle pattern. London, 1867, Lias Bros. Courtesy M. McAleer.*

Fish Eaters
Most examples date from the second half of the nineteenth century through to the present day, though earlier examples may occasionally be found.

The majority of fish knives and forks have knife handles of either ivory, mother-of-pearl or loaded silver. Solid-handle examples date mostly from the late nineteenth century onwards.

Fish services were frequently produced in quite individual designs in cased sets, particularly in the nineteenth and early twentieth century. Today most fish eaters are made to match flatware services.

See Figures 371-373.

Pitfalls
Always wash the fish eaters immediately after use to stop stains forming (see also p. 183).

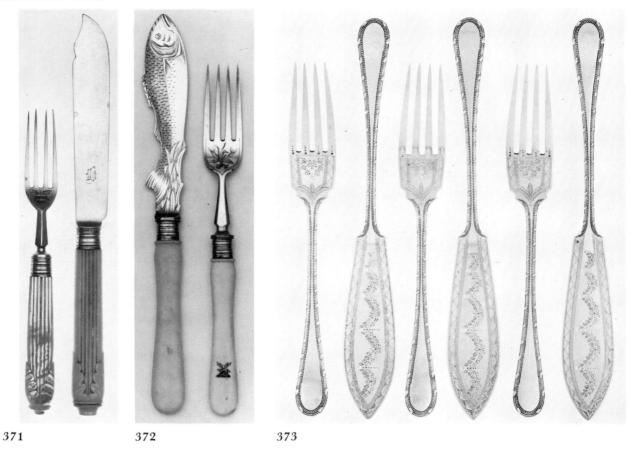

371   372   373

Figure 371. *Ivory-handled fish knife and fork of conventional form. Sheffield, 1909/10, James Dixon. Courtesy Sotheby's.*

Figure 372. *Ivory-handled fish knife and fork. A pair from a set of twelve unusual Victorian fish eaters. Birmingham, 1874, Elkington & Co. Courtesy Sotheby's.*

Figure 373. *Fish eaters with solid handles. Part of a set of twelve. Sheffield, 1898, Thomas Bradbury & Sons. Courtesy Sotheby's.*

Grapefruit Spoons

A recent (c.1900) addition to the range of flatware, distinguished from ordinary teaspoons by their bowl fronts being elongated and pointed.

Not illustrated.

Ice Cream Spoons (ice spades)

The majority date from the Regency and later nineteenth century, and are distinguished by their bowls which are either oblong shaped (easily mistaken for moist (demerara) sugar spoons) or of conventional shape with a flat base (Figure 374).

When found, these unusual and scarce spoons are normally in one of the nineteenth century flatware patterns.

See also p. 185 and Figure 325.

Pitfalls

Confusion with moist sugar spoons (p. 198). Bear in mind that ice cream spoons

Figure 374. *Ice cream spoons, part of a silver-gilt set of eighteen in Bacchanalian pattern. London, 1888, Wakely & Wheeler. Courtesy Sotheby's.*

were made in sets, whereas moist sugar spoons were usually made individually. When deciding which is which, remember that the ice cream spoon is an eating implement whereas the moist sugar spoon is for serving and usually has a much more pronounced angle from bowl to stem.

Iced-tea Spoons

A recent, late nineteenth century addition to the range of flatware, made particularly for the American market. Distinguished from ordinary teaspoons by their much longer stems. Individual examples could be mistaken for pickle spoons.

Not illustrated.

Mash Spoons (teapot spoon)

The mash or teapot spoon (used for stirring the teapot to help mash (brew) the tea) is a rare form peculiar to Scotland. It is distinguished from an ordinary teaspoon by its longer stem.

Most examples date from the eighteenth century and are of Scottish Fiddle pattern (see p. 88).

Not illustrated.

Medicine Spoons

Although any handy and appropriate sized spoon would most often have been used for the administration of medicine, three specific types can be found:

(1) Short stemmed, usually dessert size, spoons. These date from the mid-eighteenth to the mid-nineteenth century.

(2) Double ended spoons. These are found from the mid-nineteenth century on to the early twentieth century. A variety of sizes may be found, the usual being a bit

larger than a teaspoon. (Not all of this type were necessarily used for medicinal purposes — pairs have been found in travelling sets.)

(3) Gibson patent. First produced in 1827 by Charles Gibson, these spoons have a covered bowl with hinged flap and a hollow handle. By placing the thumb over the opening at the top of the handle it was possible to control the flow of the medicine.

See Figures 375-379.

Figure 375. *Medicine spoon. A particularly fine and rare mid-eighteenth century example by Paul Callard, London, c.1755, 3½ ins. long, with its original red velvet-lined green shagreen case. The inscription reads 'Gift of the Dutchefs of Queensberry to Lady Carbery' (Catherine, daughter of Henry, Earl of Clarendon and Rochester, married Charles, 3rd Duke of Queensberry 10th March, 1720 and was the last Duchess of Queensberry. She died in 1777). Courtesy Phillips.*

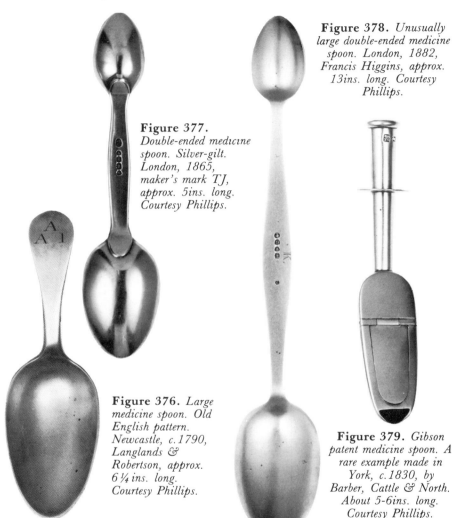

Figure 377. *Double-ended medicine spoon. Silver-gilt. London, 1865, maker's mark TJ, approx. 5ins. long. Courtesy Phillips.*

Figure 378. *Unusually large double-ended medicine spoon. London, 1882, Francis Higgins, approx. 13ins. long. Courtesy Phillips.*

Figure 376. *Large medicine spoon. Old English pattern. Newcastle, c.1790, Langlands & Robertson, approx. 6¼ ins. long. Courtesy Phillips.*

Figure 379. *Gibson patent medicine spoon. A rare example made in York, c.1830, by Barber, Cattle & North. About 5-6ins. long. Courtesy Phillips.*

Miniature Flatware

Throughout the whole period of production of flatware miniatures have been produced, some simply as toys, others scaled down for use by children. In 1771 William and Thomas Chawner supplied Parker & Wakelin with a 'childs teaspoon'. In the same year William Portal supplied a 'childs knife and fork' (Garrard Mss., Workmen's Ledger No. 2, Victoria and Albert Museum).

Miniature flatware is known by David Clayton, the most prolific of all early eighteenth century silver toy makers.

See Figures 380 and 381.

Pitfalls

When an individual spoon is found it is sometimes impossible to know whether it was originally a miniature or say a snuff spoon (see Snuff Spoons p. 215).

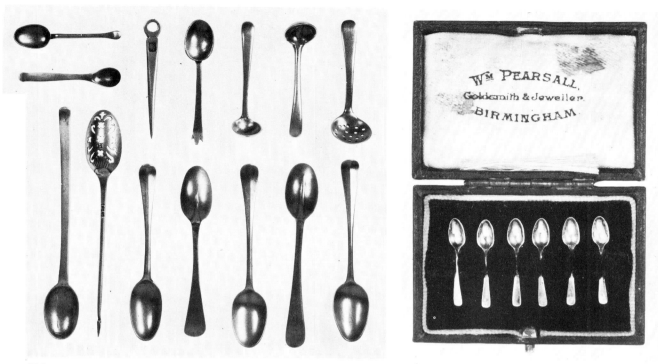

380

381

Figure 380. *Miniature flatware of the eighteenth and nineteenth centuries. Courtesy Christie's.*

Figure 381. *Set of six unmarked miniature spoons, each about 1in. long. William Pearsall registered a mark in Birmingham in 1915. Courtesy Phillips.*

Mote Spoons

Mote spoons were produced for a period of about one hundred years from the late seventeenth century. There have been many arguments over their use.

The form, throughout, is that of a pierced bowl, usually teaspoon-sized, with a long tapering stem terminating in a point.

What of its use though? It has, in recent years, been called an olive spoon. Practical as it may be for removing olives (or any other preserve) from a jar there is no evidence either documentary or otherwise to support this idea. Similarly there is no evidence to support its use with punch.

All the evidence that we do have points to these spoons being associated with tea. Particularly important in this respect is the fact that they are found as part of eighteenth century sets of tea equipage with tea caddies, sugar boxes, spoons, sugar nippers and, on occasions, cream jugs all fitting into contemporary cases (see Figures 304 and 305).

How then were they used with tea? The most commonly held belief is that the pierced bowl was used to remove the bits, or motes, that floated on the top, while the point cleared the spout when blocked.

Even if this theory is correct it is worth looking at two other possibilities if only, in one case, to eliminate a very unlikely use. First is the idea that the tea was poured through the pierced bowl, thus using it as a tea strainer. One can only say of such an idea that it could only be suggested by a very impractical person, for to use a mote spoon in this way results in tea being splashed over the surrounding table.

The second possibility is a fascinating one and quite likely the correct one. This is that the mote spoon was in fact the early form of tea caddy spoon. Tea in the seventeenth and most of the eighteenth century was supplied in a rather crude form with large leaves and a lot of dust. With such a spoon one could scoop the tea out of the caddy then lightly tap it, thus removing most of the unwanted dust. The point would be used, as already suggested, to remove blockages from the piercing inside the pot, the length of the pointed end being just right for the teapots of the period.

To add weight to this theory it is significant that the mote spoon ceased to be produced during the 1770s when caddy spoons were first produced in any quantity. It is also worth noting that quite a few eighteenth century caddy spoons have filigree centres to their bowls which would have helped to remove dust in much the same way described above.

Having looked at the possible uses of the mote spoon let us examine the types to be found.

(1) Late seventeenth century. A simple pierced bowl with long thin stem of uniform thickness. The stem and bowl are made of two pieces, the lower end of the stem soldered on to the bowl to form a rat tail. These are usually marked on the bowl.

(2) Queen Anne and George I. Still with simple pierced bowl although scrolls start to appear. The stem and bowl are made from one piece of silver. The back of the bowl has a rat tail. The stem starts to taper. Marks are now struck on the stem, usually maker's mark twice, or maker's mark and lion or Britannia.

(3) George II/III. The bulk of examples found are from this period. The rat tail disappears and various cropped rat tails, drops, and double drops are found on the back of the bowl. It is also possible to find fancy back and picture back examples as with contemporary teaspoons. The piercing of the bowls is at its most elaborate during this period, with rococo scroll work, circles, crosses, and lines all being used. Some of the finest are engraved in addition to being pierced. Marks should be struck on the base of the stem either with maker's mark only struck once or twice, or maker's mark and sterling lion.

Variants will be found such as cast rococo examples or spoons which have only one half of the bowl pierced (very rare). These naturally add to the interest and excitement of collecting such spoons. Very rare pierced bowl 'teaspoons' may also be found in original eighteenth century sets.

See Figures 382 and 383; also Figures 300 and 301 for pierced bowl teaspoons.

Pitfalls

These are amongst the most extensively faked of all objects in English silver. A very thorough examination is therefore important. The main points to look at are, first, the general proportions of the spoon — most fakes are conversions from teaspoons and, as a result, the stem tends to be shorter and more prominently tapered than it should be. Secondly, look closely at the piercing — most fakes are too simply pierced for the period of the spoon. Remember that in the eighteenth century the craftsman had the time to perfect the decoration; the modern faker rarely has this time and he will usually do only as much as he thinks is necessary to pass the object off to an unsuspecting member of the public.

There are also pitfalls with genuine examples. The most common are splits in the bowl edges, the piercing, or the stem which must be examined carefully for existing or repaired splits. All such damage will detract from the value.

Figure 382. *Two mote spoons. Left, early eighteenth century rat tail; right, mid-eighteenth century fancy back. Courtesy Phillips.*

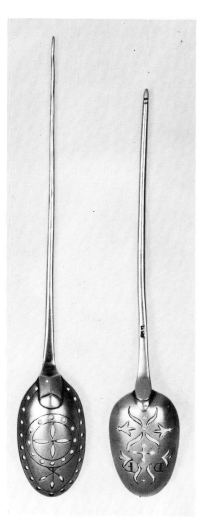

Figure 383. *Two mid-eighteenth century mote spoons. Courtesy M. McAleer.*

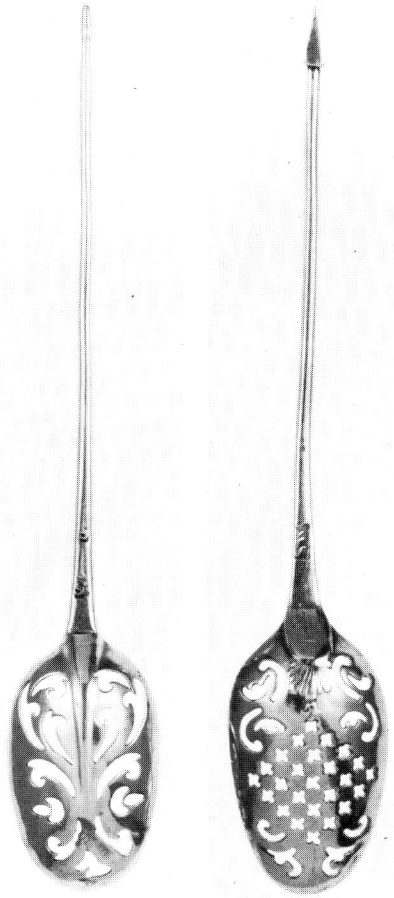

Figure 384. *Nut crackers in pierced Vine pattern. From an extensive service by Elkington. Courtesy Phillips.*

Nutcrackers

Most are nineteenth century, and the majority of examples found will be close-plated. Silver examples are rare, since there would be a tendency for them to bend, and it has been suggested that they may be for use with lobsters.

Standard flatware patterns can be found.

Regency and some later examples usually have two hinges with a short bar between, constructed in such a way that the arms can be swung round in opposite directions giving two different size gaps between them.

See Figure 384.

Picture Back and Fancy Back Spoons

With the disappearance from the backs of the bowls of spoons of the rat tail in the 1730s, the resulting plain surface presented an area for decoration, for, when the spoon was placed on the table, it was the back of the bowl which was uppermost.

Earlier on there had been decoration on the backs of bowls, the examples most frequently encountered being lace back Trefids (see Figures 73, 74 and 77). There was, therefore, nothing new in the idea of decorating the back of a spoon bowl.

The first decoration to appear in the 1730s was a rudimentary shell. This is found mostly on examples with baroque decorated stems. As the 1730s progressed and the rococo developed so the shell became more decorative and, by the mid-1740s, had become asymmetric and embellished with scrolls.

After the mid-eighteenth century pictures, as opposed to purely decorative motifs, began to appear and so the picture back evolved. These could be anything from birds to agricultural implements, the most interesting being those with political or other symbolism. Good examples of these are the heart surrounded by oak leaves with the word 'BRITISH' above for 'British hearts of oak'; the open bird cage with the bird flying out or standing on top with the words 'I LOVE LIBERTY' above (for Wilkes); and the ship symbolic of England's naval power.

Irish examples of fancy backs usually have decoration on the front of the stem.

The majority of examples to be found are teaspoons of the Hanoverian pattern, but late examples of Old English pattern may also be found. Fancy and picture back table and dessert spoons are quite scarce, and when found Hanoverian table and dessert spoons are useful in that, unlike their contemporary teaspoons, they are fully marked. Positive dating of the various motifs therefore becomes possible.

Fancy back forks are known but are rare. Basting spoons, marrow spoons, marrow scoops, mote spoons and miniatures may also be found.

The following lists give a selection of the great variety of designs which may be found on picture and fancy back spoons.

Picture backs		Fancy backs
Basket of flowers	Parrot	Shells
Vase of flowers	Squirrel	Shell and scrolls
Wheatsheaf	Stag	Scrolls
Hearts of oak	Dolphin (whale)	Ferns
Cup	Crown	Flowers
Teapot	Prince of Wales' plumes	
Farmyard scenes	Ship	
Agricultural implements	Spread Eagle	
Goose	Hearts aflame	
Dove	I love liberty	
Heron	Masonic	

See Figures 385-391.

Pitfalls

Cast fakes are a problem as are contemporary plain spoons which have had their bowls stamped into a die to produce a picture or, less often, fancy back.

The majority of such fakes are amongst the rare motifs.

When plain mid-eighteenth century spoons have their backs decorated the decoration often shows lightly inside the bowl. Normally when a picture or fancy back was made the spoon maker would allow extra thickness in the bowl where the decoration was to be stamped. A plain spoon would not have needed this extra thickness and therefore, when stamped today, the bowl does not have enough metal to carry the decoration which will show through.

Worn backs are sometimes 'improved', so always check that the condition of the bowl agrees with that of the picture.

Figure 385. *Fancy back table spoons. Notice the rudimentary shell on the 1740 example on the left, and the fully developed shell on the 1773 example on the right. Courtesy Phillips.*

Figure 386. *Fancy back marrow spoons and a scoop of the mid-eighteenth century. Courtesy Phillips.*

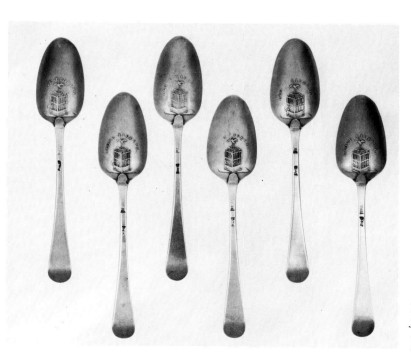

Figure 387. *'I LOVE LIBERTY', the most famous of the picture backs. Set of six teaspoons, London, c.1765, Thomas Wallis. Courtesy Phillips.*

Figure 388. *Galleon backs. Pair of table spoons, London, 1773, William Chawner. Courtesy Sotheby's.*

Figure 389. *Picture backs. Left to right, bagpipes, extremely rare, Jacobite; masonic, rare; cockerel, rare; basket of flowers. Courtesy Phillips.*

Figure 390. *Picture backs. Left to right, Prince of Wales' plumes; double headed crowned eagle; vase of flowers. Courtesy Phillips.*

Figure 391. *Picture backs. Left to right, farmyard scene; golfer, modern example; agricultural implements; squirrel on an oak stump (rare Jacobite). Courtesy Phillips.*

Snuff Spoons

Tiny spoons are known from the eighteenth century which are believed to have been for snuff. There is a problem, though, in that miniature flatware was also produced (see p. 208), so perhaps the only spoons which could properly and safely be described as snuff spoons are those actually found with snuff boxes. These are found very rarely and are in the region of 1in. in length. Slightly larger spoons are found in etuis which may also have been used for snuff.

See Figures 392 and 393.

Sucket Forks and Spoons

Most examples of these rare table implements date from the second half of the seventeenth century, though occasionally early eighteenth century ones may be found.

The spoon end is of teaspoon size; the fork is two pronged. Marks will be found on the rectangular stem which usually has a wider central panel. Individual spoons are mostly found but one rare set of five is known to exist (Figure 394).

Pitfalls

Look out for solder joins; there should not be any at any point on a sucket fork and spoon.

Figure 394. *Extremely rare set of five sucket spoons and forks. London, c.1675, maker's mark IS crowned, attributed (Kent) to John Smith. Courtesy Phillips.*

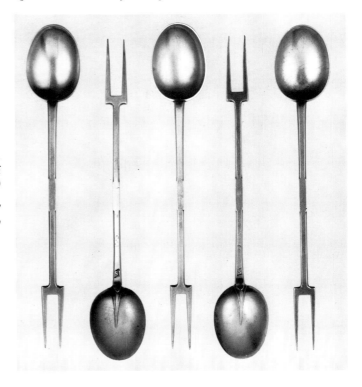

Figure 392. *Snuff (or miniature) spoon. Dog Nose pattern, c.1710. Courtesy Henry Willis.*

Figure 393. *Mid-eighteenth century etui (total length 3½ins.) with contents in place. Notice the small 'snuff' spoon on the left. Courtesy Phillips.*

Figure 395. *Late seventeenth century travelling set. The handles of the knife, fork and spoon all unscrew. Maker's mark only, FS a crown above, small s below, c.1680. Courtesy Sotheby's.*

Figure 396. *Late seventeenth century travelling set, comprising knife, fork and marrow spoon, all fitting into a filigree case, c.1680. Maker's mark only on the marrow spoon, apparently I I in a shaped shield. Courtesy Sotheby's.*

Travelling Flatware

Throughout the period of flatware production pieces have been made specifically for travelling sets. By various means these were made to be as compact as possible, the usual requirements with seventeenth and early eighteenth century examples being that they should fit into a beaker or tumbler (Figure 395) or a small case (Figure 396).

The two principal means used were either to hinge the centre of the pieces so that they would fold, or to have pieces which unscrewed in the centre.

Another fascinating type of travelling flatware found in the nineteenth century has a central stem with spoon bowls of a different size at each end. Some of these interesting and quite scarce double ended spoons were for medicine (see p. 208).

The travelling pieces most usually found are folding fruit knives, frequently and incorrectly described as pen knives and mostly dating from the late eighteenth and the nineteenth centuries. The vast majority have a silver blade which folds into a mother-of-pearl mounted covering. Less frequently forks, usually two prong, may be found. Occasionally small boxes containing both a folding knife and fork of this type come on to the market although these are quite scarce. Another rare variant has the knife blade slotting into the handle of the fork and vice versa.

Pitfalls

Worn screw threads and damaged hinges may be a problem. With mother-of-pearl mounted examples always examine for damaged or replaced mother-of-pearl.

Appendix

The Chawner & Co. Pattern Book, c.1875.

The letters H and L refer to half dies and long or full dies. It is interesting to note that most of the long die patterns date from the mid-nineteenth century and later.

Photographs courtesy C.J. Vander.

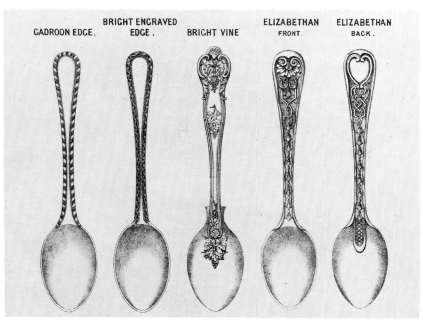

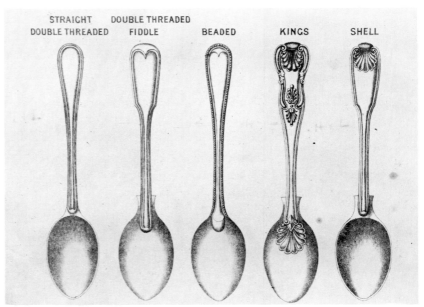

STRAIGHT DOUBLE THREADED · DOUBLE THREADED FIDDLE · BEADED · KINGS · SHELL

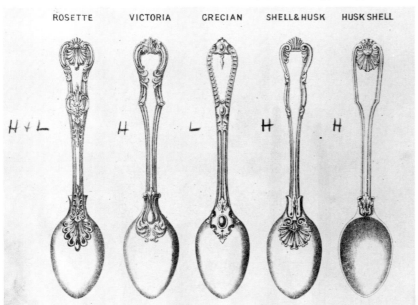

ROSETTE · VICTORIA · GRECIAN · SHELL & HUSK · HUSK SHELL

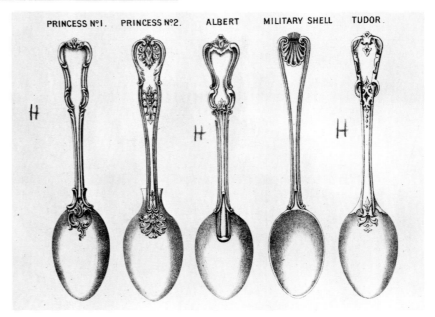

PRINCESS Nº1. · PRINCESS Nº2. · ALBERT · MILITARY SHELL · TUDOR.

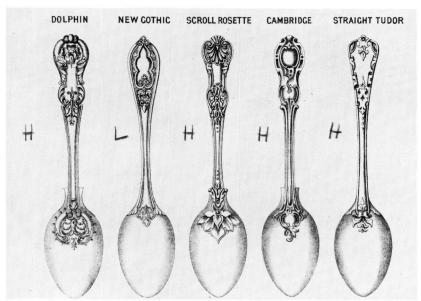

DOLPHIN	NEW GOTHIC	SCROLL ROSETTE	CAMBRIDGE	STRAIGHT TUDOR
H	L	H	H	H

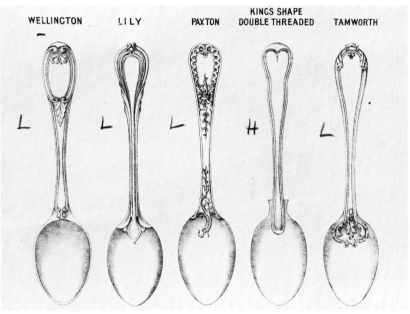

WELLINGTON	LILY	PAXTON	KING'S SHAPE DOUBLE THREADED	TAMWORTH
L	L	L	H	L

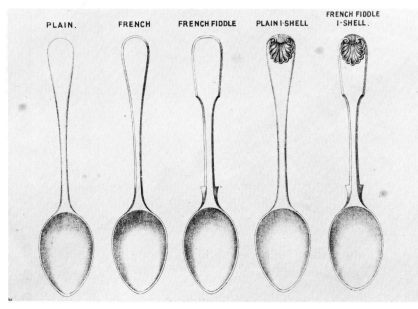

PLAIN.	FRENCH	FRENCH FIDDLE	PLAIN I-SHELL	FRENCH FIDDLE I-SHELL.

219

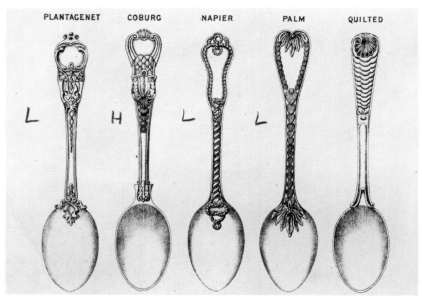

PLANTAGENET   COBURG   NAPIER   PALM   QUILTED

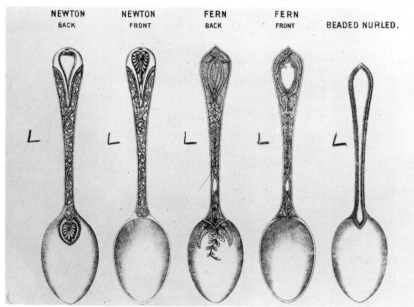

NEWTON BACK   NEWTON FRONT   FERN BACK   FERN FRONT   BEADED NURLED.

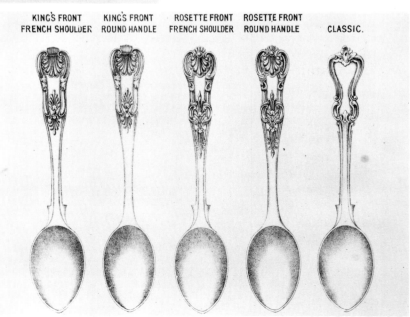

KING'S FRONT FRENCH SHOULDER   KING'S FRONT ROUND HANDLE   ROSETTE FRONT FRENCH SHOULDER   ROSETTE FRONT ROUND HANDLE   CLASSIC.

Select Bibliography

Books on spoons

Belden G., and Snodin M., *Spoons,* Pitman, 1976.

Emery, J., *European Spoons before 1700,* John Donald, 1976.

Gask, N., *Old Silver Spoons,* Herbert Jenkins, 1926; Spring Books, 1973.

How, G.E.P. and J.P., *English and Scottish Silver Spoons: Medieval to late Stuart and Pre-Elizabethan Hallmarks on English Plate,* 3 vols., printed privately, 1952-57.

Kent, T.A., *London Silver Spoonmakers 1500-1697,* The Silver Society, 1981.

Snodin, M., *English Silver Spoons,* Letts, 2nd. revised edition, 1982.

The Watchmaker, Jeweller and Silversmith, *Guide to Flatware,* 1955.

Articles on flatware

Bennet-Clark, H., 'The Importance of Taste in Plate: Sheffield Plate Flatware', *Country Life,* Feb. 1973.

Buckley, F., 'Small Silver Spoons: Emblematic Tea Spoons in the Eighteenth Century', *The Antique Collector,* Sept. and Dec. 1931.

How, G.E.P., 'The Cult of the Teaspoon', *Notes on Antique Silver,* No. 4, 1944/45.

Hughes, G.B., 'Silver Punch Ladles', *Country Life,* Nov. 1950.

Pearce, M., 'Neglected Cutlery', *Antique Collecting,* June 1979.

Pickford, I., 'Silver Flatware', *Antique Collecting,* July 1975.
   'Marrow Spoons', *Antique Collecting,* Nov. 1976.
   'Trefid Spoons and Forks', *Antique Collecting,* Dec. 1976.
   'The Hourglass Pattern', *Antique Collecting,* Feb. 1977.
   'The Dog Nose Pattern', *Antique Collecting,* May 1977.
   'Flatware', *Investing in Antiques,* Sept. 1977.
   'The Old English Pattern', *Antique Collecting,* Oct. 1977.

Smith, E.J.G., 'The English Silver Spoon', *Antique Dealer and Collectors' Guide,* Parts I-IV, March, April, May and July 1973.

Whyte, J.S., 'Scottish Georgian Silver Spoons', *Antique Collecting,* August 1969.
   'Scottish Silver Teaspoons', *Scottish Art Review,* 1969.
   'Scottish Silver Tablespoons', *Scottish Art Review,* 1967.

Catalogues

Bourdon-Smith, J.H., Ltd., *Illustrated Catalogue of Early English Spoons,* 1981.

Christie's, *Biggs Collection,* 20 Sept., 1978.

Goldsmiths Hall, *Loan Exhibition of Tea-Caddy Spoons,* 1965.

Phillips, *An Important Collection of Fancy and Picture Back Spoons,* 19 Jan., 1979.
   Alexander Collection, 9 Feb., 1979.
   A Collection of 18th Century Fancy Back Spoons, 15 June, 1979.
   Spoons, 27 June, 1980.
   Scottish Silver, 15 May, 1981.
   Private Collection, 30 Oct., 1981.
   Spoons, 18 June, 1982.

Trade Catalogues

Some of the more important examples are:

London

    Chawner & Co.

    Higgins & Son.

    The Goldsmiths and Silversmiths Company.

    C.J. Vander Ltd.

Sheffield

    James Dixon & Sons.

    John Round & Sons.

    William Hutton & Sons.

    Joseph Rodgers & Sons.

General Works

Barr, E., *George Wickes, Royal Goldsmith 1698-1761,* 1980.

Bennion, E., *Antique Medical Instruments,* 1979.

Bradbury, F., *History of Old Sheffield Plate,* 1912; reprinted 1968.

Clayton, M., *The Collector's Dictionary of the Silver & Gold of Great Britain and North America,* 1971.

Culme, J., *Nineteenth Century Silver,* 1977.

Delieb, E., *Investing in Silver,* 1967.

Edwards, A.C., *The Account Books of Benjamin Mildmay, Earl Fitzwalter,* 1977.

Himsworth, J.B., *The Story of Cutlery,* 1953.

Grimwade, A.G., *London Goldsmiths 1697-1837: Their Marks and Lives,* revised edition, 1982.

Hughes, G., *Modern Silver Throughout the World 1880-1967,* 1967.

Jackson, Sir, C.J., *An Illustrated History of English Plate,* 2 vols., 1911; reprinted 1967.

Penzer, N.M., *Paul Storr,* 1954; reprinted 1971.

Prideaux, W.S., *Memorials of the Goldsmiths' Company,* 2 vols., 1896-97.

Sheffield City Libraries, *Cutlery: a bibliography,* 1982.

Victoria and Albert Museum, *Masterpieces of Cutlery and the Art of Eating,* 1979.

Indexes

Bold figures, e.g. **178,** indicate the more important references;
italic figures, e.g. *80,* relate to figure numbers and captions.

General Index

Index of Names and Places

(Roman numerals after a name are as Grimwade's *London Goldsmiths*)

Index of Patterns and Styles